Loons

Song of the Wild

Michael Dregni, Editor
Jeff Fair and Eric Hanson, Advisory Biologists

An Anthology of Writing, Photography, and
Art From Throughout the World

With selections from Sigurd F. Olson; John James Audubon; Alexander Wilson;
Native American legends and folklore from around the world; loon researcher
Judith W. McIntyre; literary biologist Jeff Fair; and *Birder's World* editor
and publisher Eldon Greij

RAINCOAST BOOKS

Vancouver

Copyright © 1996 by Michael Dregni
Photographs copyright © 1996 by the photographers and sources noted

First published in Canada in 1996 by
Raincoast Book Distribution Ltd.
8680 Cambie Street
Vancouver, B.C. V6P 6M9
(604) 323-7100

Advisory Biologists Jeff Fair and Eric Hanson
Text edit and photo research by Todd R. Berger
Designed by Andrea Rud
Printed in Hong Kong

96   97   98   99   00   5   4   3   2   1

Canadian Cataloguing in Publication Data
Main entry under title:
Loons
     ISBN 1-55192-018-2
     1. Loons. 2. Loons—Pictorial works. I. Dregni, Michael, 1961– II. Title.
QL696.G33L66 1996   598.4'42   C95-911176-X

First published in the United States in 1996 by Voyageur Press, Inc.
123 North Second Street, P.O. Box 338, Stillwater, MN 55082 U.S.A.
612-430-2210, fax 612-430-2211

Frontis: *An adult common loon with two chicks riding on its back swims in the golden glow of a morning sunrise.* (Photo © Gregory M. Nelson)

Page 2: *Following an early morning flight in June, an adult common loon stretches its wings after landing on a Michigan lake.* (Photo © Gregory M. Nelson)

Permissions

We have made every effort to determine original sources and locate copyright holders of the excerpts in this book. Grateful acknowledgment is made to the writers and publishers listed below for permission to reprint material copyrighted or controlled by them. Please bring to our attention any errors of fact, omission, or copyright, so we may correct them in subsequent editions.
Fair, Jeff. Adapted for Voyageur Press from "Last Call?" *Equinox.* Sept./Oct. 1994. Reprinted by permission of the author.
Greij, Eldon. "Taking a Dive." *Birder's World*, June 1995. Copyright © 1995 by Eldon Greij. Reprinted by permission of the author.
Gruchow, Paul. *Travels in Canoe Country*. Boston: Bulfinch Press, 1992. Reprinted by permission of Little, Brown and Company.
McIntyre, Judith W. *The Common Loon: Spirit of Northern Lakes*. Minneapolis: University of Minnesota Press, 1988. Copyright © 1988 by the University of Minnesota. Reprinted by permission of the publisher.
Olson, Sigurd F. *Listening Point*. New York: Alfred A. Knopf, Inc., 1958. Copyright © 1958 by Sigurd F. Olson. Reprinted by permission of the publisher.

Contents

The Song of the Wild

Naturalist Sigurd F. Olson may have understood the loon's power best. Olson devoted his life to studying and preserving the northwoods and the bird that he saw as symbolic of the north: the loon. He wrote of the majesty of the loon in his memoir, *Listening Point*, writing in a simple yet insightful, poetic style, evoking the smell of the pines, the blue of the northern sky, and the call of the enchanting loon that he heard as the song of the wild.

The aim of this book is to understand the spirit of the loon through the writings of those who knew this wonderful bird most intimately. This book is an anthology of current scientific research, poetic musings of early ornithologists, writings of literary naturalists, and ages-old legends and folklore, as well as contemporary photography, early engravings, and cultural artifacts. It reflects how the loon has been observed, understood, and imagined from a time when stories were passed on by word of mouth to today, when birding field guides and scientific journals explain the bird's anatomy, physiology, and behavior.

But rather than shuffle all of the old legends and their explanations of the loon into a final chapter of quaint and curious "folk beliefs," these stories are blended together with scientific and literary writings to offer a picture of the loon as understood by a variety of cultures in differing historical contexts. A Native American legend or a Siberian folktale describes the loon in relation to their culture—that people's own "ornithology," as it were. After all, biology is the study of life, and "life" means different things to different people.

Legends surround the loon. It is a mysterious bird that evokes reverence today just as it did long ago. The loon's call, perhaps its most evocative and recognized signature, is a primeval sound that can recall simpler times and send a shiver down your spine on a warm summer evening. With a magical power like this, it is little wonder that the loon is so rich in story.

In fact, there are probably more legends explaining the loon than there are modern-day research studies. While we today do not understand the scientific "reason" for the loon's scarlet-red eyes, Inuit people of the Arctic believed that the loon's eyes were a sign of its powers of vision. In addition to seeing its way underwater to guide the soul to the spirit world, a loon could also restore eyesight to the blind. Who is to say that one understanding of the loon and its behavior may be more true than another for a certain person of a particular time and place?

Today, amid the overwhelming static of modern life, we are more inclined to believe the scientific explanation, rather than even lending an ear to the myth. But stop for a moment and listen some evening to the loon's tremolo call, and you will likely agree that the legends and the scientific research enrich each other and provide a greater understanding of the power of the loon.

Red-Throated Loon on Nest
Reflected in the still waters of Camden Bay on the Arctic coast of Alaska, a red-throated loon prepares to incubate its eggs during the long summer days and nights of continuous sunlight. (Photo © Tom Walker)

Creation of the Loon

The loon is a mysterious bird. Its cry, its red eyes, its solitariness—all combine to weave a spell around this bird, a feeling that the loon is almost primordial, and at the same time, eternal.

The mystery surrounding the loon is partly based on fact. But it is also seasoned with large doses of myth and folklore, inspired by the aura the loon's presence creates. The loon boasts a long lineage, originating from one of the most venerable families of birds still in existence, yet it is no older than several other ancient groups of birds such as ducks, storks, cranes, and grebes. Fossils of the earliest known loon, the *Colymboides anglicus,* were found in England and date from the middle Eocene epoch, some fifty million years ago. With this long lineage, it is no surprise that the loon was often the first bird recorded in the journals and daybooks of fledgling ornithologists.

And God said, "Let the water teem with living creatures, and let birds fly above the earth across the expanse of the sky." So God created the great creatures of the sea and every living and moving thing with which water teems, according to their kind, and every winged bird according to its kind. And God saw that it was good. God blessed them and said, "Be fruitful and increase in number and fill the water in the seas, and let the birds increase on earth."
—Book of Genesis, 1:20–22

Loon Up from the Depths
An adult common loon surfaces from a dive and shakes the water from its wings in the midst of a lake as the sun rises through the morning mist. Creation stories around the world—from the Ainu of Japan to Native peoples of Mongolia and Siberia to Native Americans—tell of the loon as the "Earth-Diver." In these stories, the loon dives to the depths of a flooded world and brings back a bit of earth in its beak to create the first land. (Photo © Gregory M. Nelson)

Folktales and stories of the loon tell of even earlier times, back to the very beginnings of life on Earth. Across the northern hemisphere, creation legends feature the loon as the Earth-Diver, swimming to the bottom of the great sea covering the earth to bring up the first dry land.

THE EARTH-DIVER

The Earth-Diver creation story is told with variations, reflecting the different cultures of the north. The Inuit (Eskimo), Wyandot (Huron), Iroquois, Atsina (Gros Ventre), Cree, and Arapaho peoples, among others, all retain the story. Versions of the legend are also told by the Ainu, the first people of Japan who now live on the northern Japanese island of Hokkaido; the Altaic-speaking tribes of Mongolia; and native peoples of Siberia and the Arctic regions of European Russia.

In many tellings, the loon is the central figure in the story, but some versions speak of a cormorant, duck, raven, dove, or even a turtle in the loon's stead. The Earth-Diver story is fascinating, as it includes a great ocean or flood covering the earth, a theme that appears in mythology, folklore, and religious texts of many parts of the world.

IN THE BEGINNING, all was water. There was no land nor living beings; everywhere there was the primordial water.

From the heavens above all the water, the Creator made a beautiful black and white bird, the Loon, and sent the bird as an emissary to make earth. Thus was the Loon the first act of creation.

Loon descended from the heavens, soaring downward in a spiral on its great wings until it came to the water. Loon dove into the water with its wings tucked back and propelling itself with its webbed feet. It dove as deep as it could into the depths to try to bring up mud to make the world. Loon dove twice, but it could not reach the bottom.

On its third and final dive, Loon was able to grasp just a bit of mud in its beak and swim back to the surface. That little bit of mud was enough to make land, and from the Loon's deed came forth all of the earth.

THE LOON SAVES THE WORLD

Another version of the Earth-Diver story features the loon saving the people of the world from a great flood. This story was recorded from a Lenni Lenape (Delaware) storyteller in the mid-1800s.

LONG AGO, ALL of the world was washed under water by a huge flood. The few people that survived took refuge on the back of an ancient turtle. These people lived on the turtle's back, while scanning the watery world for any signs of land, but they saw none.

One day, Loon flew by, and the people called to it and asked it to dive to the bottom of the water and bring up land. Loon complied. It dove deep into the waters but found no bottom.

So Loon flew away in search of land. It was gone for many days and traveled far and wide. Finally, Loon returned with a small trace of earth in its bill. Guided by Loon, the ancient turtle swam to the place where Loon had found dry land. There the survivors settled and re-peopled the land.

THE MAKING OF THE WORLD

Another variation of the creation story also features the loon in its role as the Earth-Diver. This story was told by the Wyandot tribe of Canada, recorded in 1874.

IN THE BEGINNING there was nothing but water, a wide sea that was inhabited by the various animals that live in and upon the water. It so happened then that a women fell down from the upper world. Although styled a woman, she was in truth a divine personage, a goddess. Two loons, which were flying over the water, happened to look up and see her fall. To save her from drowning in the waters, they caught her on their backs, and floated on the water with the divine being resting upon them.

With their loud cry, the loons called for all of the other creatures of the sea to assemble. The turtle came at their summons and relieved the loons of their burden. The water animals then held a council and decided that the divine person must have earth to live on. The animals took turns diving to the bottom of the sea to bring up earth—the beaver, the muskrat, the duck, the frog—but they all failed.

Then a loon dove, and after remaining below the water for a long time, it came back to the top, almost dead with exhaustion, but carrying a bit of earth in its beak. This earth was enough to create land. The land grew and expanded on every side, creating a great country. All of this land was carried by the turtle, which still supports the burden of the earth on its back to this day.

Now it so happened that when the divine women fell, she was pregnant with twins. Even before these twins were born, one was good and the other was evil. The good one was born in the usual way, but the evil one refused this and burst through its mother's side. This killed the divine woman, and she was buried on the new earth, and from her body sprang forth all of the vegetation on land.

The two sons went on to wage war against each other. They fought and battled, intent on destroying the other. Finally, they challenged each other to a duel. The fighting was horrible and lasted many days until finally the good son destroyed the evil one, and the good son went on to prosper on earth.

THE ANCESTORS OF THE LOON

*T*he loon originates from one of the oldest surviving families of birds. The modern loon evolved about ten million years ago from even more ancient ancestors. But while loons may sound and look primitive, they are actually highly specialized birds.

Loons are believed to share common ancestry with penguins, gulls, and albatross. And while we think of loons as an "old" bird, it is not as commonly believed *the* oldest bird.

Loons are about as old as other ancient groups of birds such as ducks, storks, cranes, and grebes.

Presently, the earliest undisputed fossil remains of a known bird are that of *Archaeopteryx*, found in Bavaria, Germany, and dating from the Jurassic Period, about 136 to 190 million years ago. *Archaeopteryx* had wings and also boasted a set of teeth. *Archaeopteryx* had solid bones like today's loon, but it probably could not fly.

The second-oldest known bird is *Gallornis straelini*, a gooselike bird that was as large as today's ostrich. *Gallornis straelini* was found in France, and lived during the Cretaceous Period of 65 to 136 million years ago. Other birds of the

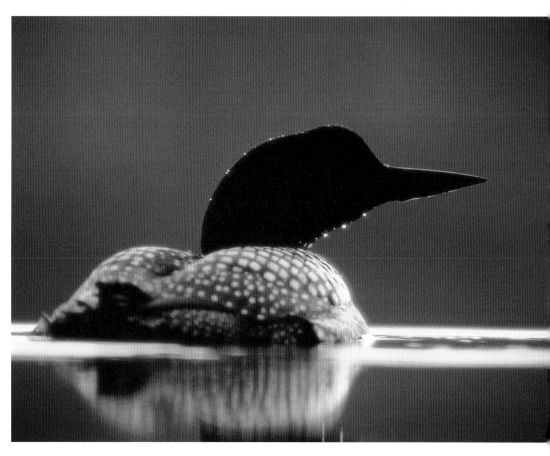

Loon in Chiaroscuro
An Anishinabeg legend holds that the first act in the creation of the world was the voice of the Spirit-Creator calling across the void to become embodied in the cry of the loon. As the Sun then rose out of the darkness, the first light distinguished itself from the darkness and became embodied in the black and white plumage of the loon. (Photo © Dr. Scott Nielsen)

Cretaceous Period include the small, toothed, gull-like *Ichthyornis*; the flightless, diving bird *Baptornis*, believed to be related to today's grebe; and the swimming bird, *Hesperornis*.

Some scientists believe the loon to be related to *Hesperornis*; others disagree. Many do agree, however, that the two shared some traits. *Hesperornis* looked like a loon and was adapted to swimming and diving, but it was seven feet long and flightless. It ate fish like the loon but had teeth in its bill like *Archaeopteryx*. The bone structure of the wings and legs of *Hesperornis* differed greatly from the modern loon, and despite the many similarities between the birds, the scientific evidence linking them is inconclusive.

The earliest fossil remains of a loon are that of the *Colymboides anglicus*, which lived in England fifty million years ago during the middle Eocene Epoch. The next-oldest loon remains are that of *Colymboides minutus*, found in France and dating to the late Oligocene or early Miocene Epochs, some twenty to thirty million years ago. Fossil records of other loonlike species from the Pliocene Epoch of about two to six million years ago have been found in Italy, the former Czechoslovakia, and in North America in Florida and California.

Fossil remains of all five of our modern loon species originate from the Pleistocene Epoch of two million to ten thousand years ago. During this epoch, glacial ice was widespread, and modern human beings are believed to have evolved. Scientists believe that it was during this relatively late time period that a group of common loons may have become separated by glaciers, leaving one isolated group in the Arctic and another larger group further south. The divergence of the species eventually resulted in a new species in the Arctic regions: the yellow-billed loon.

Pleistocene loon fossils were found in the Old Crow Basin in Canada's northern Yukon Territory, an area that is in the range of the common, red-throated, Pacific, and yellow-billed loons today. Fossils of a Pacific loon were uncovered at the site in beds more than fifty-four thousand years old while fossils of the red-throated and the yellow-billed loons were at least ten thousand years old.

So whether the loon brought the earth up from the depths or simply evolved like the rest of us, it remains a mysterious bird with a call that evokes the beginning of time and the song of all that is wild.

Common Loon at Sunrise
Above: *An adult common loon swims into the morning sunrise carrying two chicks on its back. Carrying chicks on their backs is a loon trait that gave rise to the mistaken folk belief that loons hatched their young from under their wings and carried them hidden away beneath their feathers until they were several days old.* (Photo © Gregory M. Nelson)

Call of the Pacific Loon
Facing page: *A Pacific loon calls its timeless cry across the waters of Alaska. Many stories have been told on how the loon got its cry. The Algonquins of Maine and Newfoundland believed that Loon was a messenger of their legendary hero, Glooscap, who taught Loon its cry. Long ago, Glooscap came to visit the people; when it was time to leave, the people pleaded with him not to go as they were lonely. Glooscap felt sorry for them and so gave Loon its cry so it could summon his spirit whenever the Algonquins were in need. The cry Glooscap taught the loon was a special call that simultaneously sounded as though it were nearby and far away.* (Photo © Gary L. Lackie)

Wingflap

Above: *A common loon flaps its wings on a foggy morning. The origin of the loon's plumage is explained in an Inuit story about the old days when all birds were white. Loon and Raven agreed to tattoo each other using their beaks and the black ashes from a fire. Raven tattooed Loon first, creating the beautiful black and white pattern across Loon's back. But when it came time for Raven to be tattooed, he was too impatient, and Loon threw the ashes all over Raven, coating him in black.* (Photo © Gregory M. Nelson)

Loon Spirit Mask

Facing page: *An Inuit ceremonial mask of a loon, carved from wood in the 1980s by Edward Kiokun, an Alaskan Inuit from Nunivak Island. Masks were used in Inuit festivals and were originally carved by shamans. According to Edward William Nelson's ethnography* The Eskimo About Bering Strait, *published in 1896–1897, the Inuit believed that all animate beings led a dual existence, becoming at will either human or animal. The humanlike form is called the* inua *and represents the cognitive aspect of the creature; at death, the* inua *becomes the animal's "shade," or spirit. The* inua *is shown on this mask in the central painting of a human head, done in red ochre. Shamans could see through the animal to its human features, and people who wore the masks in a ceremony became possessed by the animal's spirit. This mask measures twenty-four inches (60 cm) from the tail to the beak. Around the body are separate appendages—webbed feet, fish, and wings—held by dowels and sinew.* (Courtesy of the Alaska State Museum, Juneau, Catalog # II-A-1457)

Naming the Loon

The loon has been known by many names, from the descriptive terms of early Native cultures to the first efforts of ornithologists to classify all of the world's avian species. The names tagged to the loon represent a mixture of myth and science, legend and folklore.

The Lord did well when he put the loon and his music in the land.
—**Aldo Leopold**

Not surprisingly, the naming of the loon in both popular and scientific realms has focused on several of the most fascinating aspects of the bird. People from different parts of the world have named the loon after its call, based on a phonetic version of the loon's mew or its startling tremolo. Others have labeled the bird after its most intriguing or distinctive physical characteristics, including the color of its beak, the throat feathers, or its plumage patterns.

Some cultures have labeled the loon based on superstitions. The names ember goose, rain goose, and Calls-Up-A-Storm all highlight a society's respect for this mysterious bird.

Red-Throated Loon
In some regions of the elegant red-throated loon's range, people believe that the bird can prophesize the coming of rain or stormy weather and warn the world with its strange call. People from the Shetland Islands know the red-throated loon as the Rain Goose for its ability to foretell—and even bring on—rain. The bird was christened with the scientific classification Gavia stellata. Gavia *signifies the loon's genus;* stellata *is Latin for "starred," as early observers believed that they saw the shape of a star in the bird's deep-red throat patch. (Photo © Tom Walker)*

NAMING NAMES

Native people of the Arctic named the loon for both its physical features and its cry, the most distinguishing characteristics of the bird. The Inuit call it *tuu'lik* or *too-lick*, translating as "having a tusk," or *tasingik*, meaning "black-billed," both in reference to its long, black bill. The Anishinabeg, also known as the Ojibwe or Chippewa, call it *mahng* and believed that the loon was brave of heart.

Beginning in the 1700s, European ornithologists classified the loon according to the scientific binomial nomenclature originated in the middle part of the century by Swedish botanist Carolus Linnaeus. Linnaeus originally gave the loon the genus *Colymbus*, derived from the medieval German word *Kolymbis*, or "diving bird." In the 1800s, French naturalist Baron Georges Cuvier classified the loon in the genus *Urinator*, Latin for "diver" and pertaining to "tail-swimmer" birds. This classification, however, was never widespread, and Linnaeus' nomenclature was preferred by many ornithologists up until the twentieth century. Loons have also been at times considered part of the orders *Pygopodes* ("rump-feet" birds) and *Cecomorphs* ("shaped like a seabird"). These classifications were descriptive of the loon's anatomy and aptitude for diving, but they have also fallen out of favor with ornithologists.

The current classification is odd at best. Today, the loon is categorized in the order *Gaviiformes*, family *Gaviidae*, genus *Gavia*. *Gavia* is Latin for "gull" and was bestowed on the loon by German naturalist Johann Reinhold Forster during his around-the-world travels with Captain James Cook in the late 1700s. This eccentric nomenclature survived and sustains a token of the loon's confused classification history; in different guides and birding manuals down through the centuries, the loon was grouped with species of mews, mergansers, auks, and grebes, among other waterfowl. Despite the gull-inspired scientific name, the loon is recognized today as a separate order comprising only five species and one subspecies.

THE FIVE LOONS

The five species in the loon genus make up a relatively small family when compared with most groups of birds. The five species are the common loon, Arctic loon, Pacific loon, yellow-billed loon, and red-throated loon.

The common loon was originally called *Colymbus glacialis* by Linnaeus in 1764, and later known as *Colymbus immer*. It is classified today as *Gavia immer*, from the Latin *immergo*, "to immerse," or *immersus*, "submerged." The name "*immer*" also relates to an old popular name in northern Europe for the common loon—ember goose—which originated in legends describing the creation of the distinctive coloration of the loon through a dousing in ashes and embers.

Linnaeus originally classified the Arctic loon as *Colymbus arcticus* in 1758. It is known today as *Gavia arctica*. *Arctica* is Latin for "northern." The Arctic loon and Pacific loon were long considered a single species by North American scientists, but in the Soviet Union, the primary range of the Arctic loon, they had been considered separate species. In 1985, the American Ornithologists' Union classified the Arctic and Pacific loons as distinct species, with the newly designated Pacific loon known as *Gavia pacifica*. The sole recognized loon subspecies is the east Siberian Arctic loon (*Gavia arctica viridigularis*), a subspecies of *Gavia arctica*.

The yellow-billed loon was classified as *Colymbus adamsi*, named in 1859 by British zoologist G. R. Gray in honor of Edward Adams, a British naval surgeon, polar explorer, and collector of natural history specimens. It is known today as *Gavia adamsii*.

Danish naturalist Bishop Erik Pontoppidan first classified the red-throated loon as *Colymbus stellatus* in 1763. It is known today as *Gavia stellata*, after the Latin for "starred." Pontoppidan believed he saw a red star in the loon's throat patch.

POPULAR NAMES FOR THE LOON

The popular names given to the loon over time are varied and colorful, reflecting the broad geographic range of the loon across cultures, as well as the legends and observations of extremely diverse societies.

In the British Isles, the genus is aptly known as the dipper or diver. At times, it was also known as a dabchick, or even Hell-diver for its ability to dive to unknown depths. The French name for the loon, *plongeon*, also translates as diver.

Great Northern Divers by J. G. Keulemann
Called the common loon in North America, the bird is known as the great northern diver in the United Kingdom. Nature artist J. G. Keulemann illustrated an adult "diver" in summer (foreground) and winter plumage posed before an iceberg. The illustrations appeared in Henry E. Dresser's grand natural history guidebook, A History of the Birds of Europe, *published in 1871–1881. (Courtesy of the Minneapolis Athenaeum at the Minneapolis Public Library)*

In North America, it is called the loon, a term that bears many different meanings and a varied etymology. The name is thought to derive from an old term from Scandinavia, *løm*, meaning a lame or clumsy person, akin to the English term *lubber, lumme,* or *lummox.* This etymology reflects the bird's clumsiness on land—a land lubber. This parallels one of the old scientific classifications for the bird, *Pygopodes* or "arsefoot," relating to the placement of the loon's legs far back on its body, which facilitates swimming and diving but hampers its walk.

The word "loon" also has doubled for "fool," as William Shakespeare used in *Othello*: "The devil damn thee black, thou cream-fac'd loon!" Again, the term was probably attached to the bird because of its awkwardness on land.

"Loon" may also have derived from lunatic, which in turn came from the Latin *luna*, or "moon," as many people believed that the phases of the moon affected the mad. According to this etymology, the call of the loon probably earned it the name. As naturalist writer John McPhee notes of the loon's call, "If he were human, it would be the laugh of the deeply insane."

Other popular names used throughout the world are based on the bird's cry. The Russian name for the loon *gagára* and the Finnish name for the Arctic loon *kuikka* are both phonetic versions of the bird's song. Perhaps the most evocative loon name is the moniker used by the Québecois, *huart à collier*, translating as "cry in a necklace."

POPULAR NAMES OF THE INDIVIDUAL SPECIES

The divergence of popular names continues among the five species of the loon. Common names for the loon species typically describe the distinguishing features of the birds, as well as their behavior, characteristics, and once again, their call.

The common loon is also known as the big loon, black-billed loon, ring-necked loon, walloon, ember goose, immer goose, imber or ember diver, greenhead, and guinea duck; in Great Britain, it is commonly called the great northern diver. In Norway and Sweden it was also called the *islom*, or ice loon,

as it did not migrate until the water turned to ice. The Gaelic name for the bird is *mur bhuachaille*, or sea herdsman.

The Arctic loon is also known as the black-throated loon and green-throated loon; in the British Isles it is called the Arctic diver or black-throated diver.

The Pacific loon is sometimes known as the purple-throated loon due to the purple highlights of its neck plumage.

The red-throated loon is also known as the little loon, cape drake, cape racer, cobble, pepper-shinned loon, and scape grace; in the British Isles, it is commonly called the red-throated diver. Other nicknames such as pegging-awl loon came from the shape of its beak, likened to a cobbler's awl. The British also called it the sprat loon or spratoon, coming from its love of sprat, a type of small herring.

The yellow-billed loon is known in Great Britain as the white-billed diver, white-billed northern diver, or as the Adams' diver, in reference to its scientific name, *Gavia adamsii*.

THE LOON DURING ADVENT WEEK

The common loon has been known as the immer goose. Oddly enough, due to its hardship in walking, the bird once gave its name to the final Sunday in the Christian Advent.

The naturalist Bishop Erik Pontoppidan wrote in the nineteenth century of the "immer goose" that "Its wings are so short, it can hardly raise itself with them; and its legs are so far back that they are not so much used to walk with as to paddle along the water on which account the Immer is never seen to come ashore, excepting in the week before Christmas, wherefore the fourth Sunday in Advent is called by the people Immer, or as the people express it, Ommer Sunday."

This archaic term is no longer in widespread use.

THE RAIN GOOSE

In many parts of the northern world, the loon is considered a prophet of the weather. From Norway to Canada's Pacific coast, the loon's call is thought to signal rain. As the

Loon Performing Wingflap
To finish their preening, loons often douse themselves with water and then "stand" in the water, flapping their wings to ruffle their feathers back into place.
(Photo © Bruce Montagne)

ornithologists Alexander Wilson and Charles Lucian Bonaparte noted in their legendary guide *American Ornithology*, "The loon is restless before a storm; and an experienced master of a coasting vessel informed me, that he always knew when a tempest was approaching by the cry of this bird, which is very shrill, and may be heard at the distance of a mile or more. The correctness of this observation I have myself since experienced in a winter voyage on the coasts of the United States."

John James Audubon scoffed at such beliefs. While voyaging from Charleston, South Carolina, to the Florida Keys in 1832, he wrote: "There is an absurd notion, entertained by persons unacquainted with the nature of this bird, that its plaintive cries are a sure indication of violent storms. Sailors in particular, are ever apt to consider these call-notes as por-

tentous. . . . I several times saw and heard loons traveling eastward; but not withstanding all the dire forebodings of the crew, who believed that a hurricane was at hand, our passage was exceedingly pleasant."

Nevertheless, in the Shetland Islands, the long, harsh call of the red-throated loon—*kark, kark, kakera,* as phonetically deciphered by Howard Saunders in his *Manual of British Birds*—is thought to warn of wet or stormy weather. Thus the red-throated loon is widely known to Shetlanders as the "rain goose."

Along the coast of British Columbia, Native cultures believed in the call of the common loon as a predictor of rain. In addition, they believed the loon could actually cause rain with its cry. For this ability, the loon was known as Calls-Up-A-Storm.

The Loon on Land and in the Sky

The loon is indeed an ill-shaped bird—ill-shaped for life out of the water, that is. The loon could better be described as an *odd*-shaped bird, at least in comparison with many other birds. Its "shape" is the result of centuries of evolution that have fashioned a bird that is perhaps *ideally* shaped for living in water.

The five species of loons largely share their shape as well as many features and much behavior, yet there are also eccentricities among the species. Red-throated loons, for instance, are the only loons that can take wing from land; all others must take off from water. Contrary to typical avian biannual molting, loons molt their flight feathers only once a year—except the red-throated loon, which does molt its flight feathers twice.

Common Loon on Nest
A common loon rests on its nest by a Michigan lake in June, incubating eggs. As its physiology is designed for diving, the loon's legs are set far back on its body, leaving the bird almost incapable of walking on land—"terrestrially helpless," as a Soviet ornithologist wrote. Thus, loons typically build their nests close to the waterline so they can slip easily into the safety of the water if they feel threatened. (Photo © Gregory M. Nelson)

SUCH IS THE LOON

Ornithologist Edward Howe Forbush described the loon with beautiful 1920s-period poetry that is a far cry from today's cold and exacting scientific guidebook description. This excerpt from his guide *Birds of Massachusetts and Other New England States* (1929) is inspired by a true bird lover's admiration of the loon:

THE LOON IS a wonderful, powerful, living mechanism fashioned for riding the stormy seas. See him as he mounts high above the waves, neck and legs fully extended "fore and aft," and bill a trifle raised which gives to his whole form a slight upward bend, his wings beating powerfully and moving as steadily as the walking-beam of a side-wheel steamship. He is driving straight ahead into the teeth of the gale and making greater headway than the laboring steamer that steers a parallel course. Now he slants downward, and striking just beyond the top of a towering wave shoots down its inclined surface and rises again on the coming crest. Here, midway of the wide bay where the seas are running high and wildly tossing their white tops, with a wintry gale whipping the spray from them in smoky gusts, the Loon rests at ease, head to the wind and sea like a ship at anchor. The tossing and the tumult disturb him not, as he rides, light as a birch canoe, turning up his white breast now and then on one side as he reaches unconcernedly backward to preen his feathers. His neck narrows at the water-line into a beautifully modeled cutwater. His broad paddles push his white breast to the tops of the great waves, where it parts the foam as he surmounts the crests and glides easily down into the gulfs beyond. The freezing spray that loads the fishing fleet with tons of ice seems never to cling to his tough and glossy plumage; or if it does, he washes if off among the fleeing fishes away down in the warmer currents near the bottom of the bay.

Often toward nightfall I have heard his wild storm-call far out to windward against the black pall of an approaching tempest like the howl of a lone wolf coming down the wind; and have seen his white breast rise on a wave against the black sky to vanish again like the arm of a swimmer lost in the stormy sea. Sailors, hearing the call, say that the loons are trying to blow up an "easterly." At times his cries seem wailing and sad as if he were bemoaning his exile from his forest lake. Such is the Loon in his winter home off our coast; for there he lives and braves the inclemency of the season. Of all the wild creatures that persist in New England, the Loon seems best to typify the stark wildness of primeval nature.

LAUGHING LOON

Throughout his writings, Sigurd F. Olson championed the conservation of the loon, the bird he regarded as the voice of the wilderness. Olson wore many hats throughout his lifetime: canoe guide in the Boundary Waters region of Minnesota and Canada's Quetico Provincial Park; biology professor; conservation consultant to the federal government; naturalist writer with dozens of books to his credit; and woodsman, making his home at Listening Point near Ely, Minnesota. In this excerpt from his book *Listening Point* he provides a literary and evocative natural history of the loon and its meaning to the wild world:

THE CANOE WAS drifting off the islands, and the time had come for the calling, that moment of magic in the north when all is quiet and the water still iridescent with the fading glow of sunset. Even the shores seemed hushed and waiting for that first lone call, and when it came, a single long-drawn mournful note, the quiet was deeper than before.

Above came a swift whisper of wings, and as the loons saw us they called wildly in alarm, increased the speed of their flight, and took their laughing with them into the gathering dusk. Then came the answers we had been waiting for, and the shores echoed and re-echoed until they seemed to throb with the music. This was the symbol of the lake country, the sound that more than any other typifies the rocks and waters and forests of the wilderness.

To me only one other compares with it in beauty and meaning, the howling of the husky dogs around the Indian villages in the far north. Their wild and lonely music epitomizes the far reaches of the Canadian Shield, means nights when northern lights are a blazing curtain along the horizon.

While the northern loon in startling black and white, with its necklace of silver and jet and five-foot spread of wings, is of great interest scientifically, it is the calling that all remember. Whoever has heard it during spring and summer never forgets the wild laughing tremolo of the reverberating choruses.

One such night is burned into my memory. It was moonlight, the ice had just gone out, and the spring migration was in full swing. Loons were calling everywhere, not only on Knife but on adjacent lakes, and the night was full of their music from sunset until dawn. The echoes kept the calling going until it was impossible at times to tell which was real. While I listened it seemed to me that in that confused medley of sounds was a certain harmony as though major chords were being held for periods of time. It may have been imagination, but I have heard hints of it at other times as well. On this night there was no mistake, for the calling blended with the echoes until the illusion was complete.

The weirdest call of all is the yodel somewhat similar to the break in voice and the clear bugle-like note used by humans in calling across wide valleys in the Alps. This is the danger call used when a canoe is approaching a nesting area or when invasion is imminent. It can start all the loons within hearing, and when the yodeling blends with tremolo they are really making music.

The third call is the wail often mistaken for the howl of a wolf, and of much the same quality. It rises and falls in pitch and is used when a mate is calling for relief from its brooding on the nest or when signaling the young. Just that morning we heard it among the islands. We had been watching a pair swim slowly around the little bay where they had nested, with a lone chick riding sedately upon the back of one of

Symbol of Wilderness
A common loon swims across a clear forest lake at dawn with a birch-tree-covered island in the distance. In his many books of canoe travels and nature writings, Minnesota naturalist Sigurd F. Olson wrote poetically about the loon and its cry, which he described as "the sound that more than any other typifies the rocks and waters and forests of the wilderness." (Photo © Gregory M. Nelson)

them. When they saw us, they gave their warning calls at once, for that lone chick riding so grandly around the bay and no more than a day or two off the nest was far too small to fend for itself. We paddled toward them while the calling grew more and more intense, came at last directly between the parents and their young one, which now was trying desperately to dive. A week old it would have been able to submerge and swim for fifty feet or more, but this little chap was at our mercy and the parents were aware of its danger. At times they came almost within touching distance and tried to draw us away with the old ruse of pretending to have a broken wing and thus easy to catch. How they floundered and threw themselves about. When their enticements failed to work, they approached again, rearing up on their tails and uttering loud cries as they balanced there and all but treading water before flopping forward onto their breasts. The performance was repeated over and over again. They screamed and hooted and yodeled and gave the laughing call, but to no avail, while the chick, now confused and thoroughly frightened, swam hopelessly beside the canoe. Other loons in the vicinity swiftly joined the commotion, and the entire area was in turmoil.

Deciding they had been frightened too much, we turned and paddled back to the point, but for a long time after we had gone the calling continued. It was not surprising they were alarmed, for this lone chick brought out all of their protective instincts for the season of mating and nesting. Seldom owning more than two and often only one because of predation, they found in that last chick their whole excuse for being.

Just after the ice was out we had watched that pair come into the bay, stake out their nesting area, and repel invaders whenever they approached. One day we watched the courtship. They came toward each other slowly and, as they neared, dipped their bills rapidly in the water and just as rapidly flipped them out again. This was followed by several short swift dives, exaggerated rolling preens and stretchings such as only loons seem able to do. Suddenly they broke away from such intimacy, raced off across the water, striking the surface with powerful wing beats in a long curving path that eventually led back to where they had started. All during this time they indulged in the laughing call. Sometimes in the ecstasy of display they reared high on their tails as they did when their chick was endangered, struck their snowy breasts violently on the water, then raced again around the bay. Only once did we see this, but shortly afterward the mating was over and then we found the nest in a tussock of grass on a little swampy island close to shore and facing the open water. It was placed so they could slip off swiftly and reach the deeps should danger come behind them from the shore. The two olive-brown and somewhat speckled eggs were soon laid in a small shallow depression in the grass that was built up during the days of incubation until it was a concave little mound, each mate doing its share while it sat there, pecking and adding a grass blade at a time from the vegetation within reach.

A couple of weeks later one of the eggs was destroyed by some prowler, possibly a mink, a crow or a muskrat. The remaining egg now took all of their attention, and they guarded it jealously every moment of the day and night. If this had been stolen too, it would have meant a new nest and possibly another hatching.

Struggling to Take Off
Loons appear to run awkwardly across the top of the water as they struggle to take wing. Laboring to lift off from a lake, this adult common loon thrashes the water with its wings in an awkward dash. Once in the air, the imprint of the loon's takeoff is left like a signature on the face of the lake: an easily recognized path of its long runway accented by expanding saucers of waves where its wingtips struck the water. (Photo © Gregory M. Nelson)

Reflection of the North Woods

A common loon floats amid birch trees mirrored in a northern lake. A Micmac legend holds that loons were once land birds. Invited to a great Micmac feast, Loon's wobbly walk annoyed his host, as he knocked over food and drink. The host grabbed Loon and threatened to kill him. Loon begged him to do anything but throw him in the water. The Micmac, thinking that water was Loon's great fear, tossed Loon into a lake, whereupon Loon swam happily away. And that was how the loon became a water bird. (Photo © Bruce Montagne)

Scientists say that in half the nests only one hatches out, and that the low rate of survival accounts for the fact that loons are never numerous. If two individuals reproduce themselves after their third year, then things are going well. It is surprising in view of the high mortality rate that populations remain as steady as they do, that, in spite of predation, loons are found on almost every lake in the north.

One afternoon we sat on the point watching a flock of them playing on the open water. They had been there as a group since midsummer, bachelor loons and pairs that had not nested or had lost their eggs. Now free of responsibilities, these thwarted birds gathered each morning and spent the day together in the open. It may have been that the fishing was good in that particular spot, but I am tempted to believe they got together for a companionship that took the place of nests and young.

Suddenly one of the group called and then all together until the channel before us was again full of sound. Excited by their own music, they chased one another madly across the water, returning always to the place they had left. Toward dusk the flock began to disband, single birds first and then pairs flying back, no doubt, to their abandoned nesting areas. Sometime in the morning they would drift back again by ones and twos to spend the day together as they do on many of the larger lakes all summer long.

A pair flew close to the point and settled in the bay off the beach, and we watched them diving there for minnows, timing them to see how long they could stay submerged. Seldom did one stay under for more than half a minute, but there are records of dives as long as two and three minutes in duration. Some have been recorded even longer than that, but such observers may have failed to see a partial emergence for air. They are wonderful divers and swimmers, can pursue and overtake the swiftest of fish, and it has been said a loon can dive at the flash of a gun and be under water before the bullet strikes.

They can also submerge gradually, can control specific gravity possibly by a compression of feathers and expulsion of air from the lungs until the body is approximately the same weight as the water. All divers have a high tolerance for carbon dioxide, and oxygen needs are met, not from free air in the lungs, but from the oxyhemoglobin and oxymyoglobin stored in the muscles, substances responsible for the dark color of flesh in most waterfowl. This explains the diving, the gradual sinking from sight, and the fact that they have been caught on fishermen's set lines in Lake Superior at depths of two hundred feet.

Once I sat in a canoe at Lower Basswood Falls and watched a loon fishing in the rapids not fifty feet away. Suddenly the bird dove and swam directly under the canoe not two feet below the surface. The wings were held tightly at the sides and the legs the sole means of locomotion. When a young chick is learning to swim beneath the surface it uses both legs and wings, a reversion perhaps to the days of its reptilian ancestors; a habit generally abandoned, however, when it becomes adult.

It was now much too dark to see and we left our loons for the light and warmth of the cabin, but in the morning we watched them again. The pair had stayed close to the bay during the night and now were swimming around in the sunshine, getting ready to join the gathering flock on the open lake. We watched them, the brilliant black-and-white markings on their backs, saw one preen, rolling over on its side exposing the silvery-white breast until it glittered and shone in the morning sun. The other rose to its full height, flapped its wings vigorously, and settled down again. Then both dove with scarcely a ripple to mark their descent and soon were far past the point, heading for the rendezvous.

Some say that loons eat too many fish and should be reduced in numbers, but as the population on most lakes is small, with usually only one or two per square mile of the area, this is a ridiculous assumption. To be sure, they do eat fish, but, like most predators of the type, they also eat insects, mollusks, crustacea, and even vegetation. We can well afford to keep them, for their aesthetic value far outweighs any other consideration. Without the music of their calling and the sight of them on the open water, the lakes of the north would never be the same.

A pair flew overhead, and we heard plainly the whistle of their wings, watched the slow and powerful beats as they headed across the lake. As they passed the gathering flock they gave the tremolo once and then settled down with the rest. I had hoped they might do what I had seen them do in the past, glide into the waiting group with wings set and held in a motionless V above their backs. Once I had seen them come in that way on Kekekabic, approaching the lake like seaplanes about to land in a long unbroken glide from the top of the ridge to the water's surface.

But, while they are strong flyers and can swim and dive as few birds can, they are absolutely helpless on land, and only once have I seen one more than twenty feet from water. I was coming across a portage with a canoe on my back, and there, to my amazement, was a loon standing bolt upright in the center of the trail. I was so startled by the apparition in black and white that its scream of alarm almost made me drop the canoe. The bird turned and literally hurled itself toward the shore, half flying, swimming and running on its ridiculously tiny legs. With a wild water-choked yelp it plunged into the shallows and out to diving depth and swiftly disappeared. That explained why nests are always close to the shore. Loons must be able to slide instantly into the water, cannot waste precious moments struggling over land. No creature is clumsier out of its element than this great diver of the north.

The sound of a whippoorwill means an orange moon coming up in the deep south; the warbling of meadowlarks the wide expanses of open prairies with the morning dew still upon them; the liquid notes of a robin before a rain the middle west and east; the screaming of Arctic terns the marshes of the far north. But when I hear the wild rollicking laughter of a loon, no matter where I happen to be, it means only one place in the world to me—the wilderness lake country and Listening Point.

LOON PLUMAGE AND MOLTING

Loons are streamlined birds adapted for diving, swimming, and flying. Thus, while all five species have attractive and dramatic summer plumage, none have crests, plumes, or long tails.

Oddly, adult yellow-billed, Arctic, Pacific, and common loons molt their flight feathers only once a year, half as often as almost all other birds, which typically molt in summer and in winter. Loons molt completely in winter and cannot fly during this time. In the fall, loons partially molt, shedding all but their flight feathers. Only the red-throated loon follows the typical bird cycle of molting completely twice a year.

Loon researcher Judith W. McIntyre provides an explanation for this odd behavior in her study *The Common Loon: Spirit of Northern Lakes*: "Why, if ducks molt in July, and endure a flightless period, don't loons do the same? Ducklings feed themselves, and the period of intense parental care is shorter for them than for loons. Loon chicks require nearly constant parental attention during the summer, and loonlings must be fed by their parents for nearly three months. Is it possible that the extended care period has influenced timing of the molt? Perhaps loons would not be able to provide for young and still fulfill their own metabolic requirements during molting."

Thus, loons, with the exception of the red-throated loon, wear one plumage during the winter and another through the rest of the year. From spring to fall, common loons have white bellies and black bodies covered with white spots, a black-and-white necklace, and a glossy, green-black head. In winter, they are gray brown with a white belly.

Yellow-billed loons share similar seasonal plumage with common loons, except that their feather shafts are white in contrast to the dark shafts of common loons. Their bills are yellow to white-yellow instead of the common loon's dark-colored bill. Yellow-billed loons typically carry their beaks upturned in comparison with common loons, which usually carry their beaks on the level.

Arctic and Pacific loons have similar plumage to the common loon from spring to fall, but with a light gray head. The Arctic loon's neck has a black or green-black patch whereas the Pacific loon's is black to purple-black. In winter, they both have gray-brown plumage with white bellies.

Red-throated loons in summer have white bellies and a dark gray mottled body; their heads are lighter gray with a striped black and white cap and a maroon-brown throat. In winter, they have a mottled gray back and a white throat.

LOON AND RAVEN: THE STORY OF THEIR PLUMAGE

The Inuit from Alaska to Greenland tell a story explaining how both the loon and the raven got their distinctive plumage. Several variations of the story are recorded, but in all of them the loon and the raven both receive their coloring

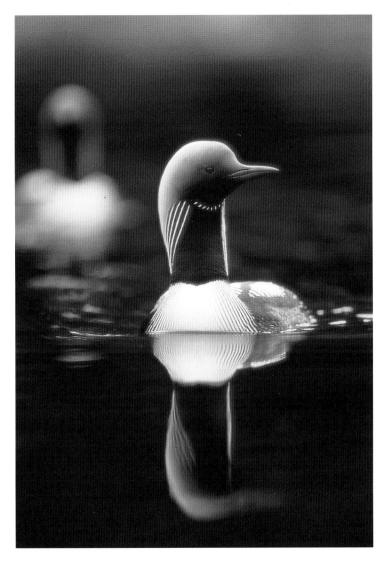

Pacific Loon
The Pacific and Arctic loons share similar plumage with the common loon, with the exception of the head feathers. These two species boast gray heads, the Pacific loon's being a light gray (as seen here) and the Arctic loon's being darker. They also both have dark-colored throat patches. The Arctic loon is sometimes called the black- or green-throated loon whereas the Pacific loon is known as the purple-throated loon, monikers reflecting the glossy highlights in their throat patches. (Photo © Gary L. Lackie)

as a result—and as a reflection—of their personalities. This version is based on a tale told by a Greenland Inuit named Autarita as transcribed by Danish polar explorer Knud Rasmussen in 1908:

DO YOU KNOW why Raven is so black, so tiresomely black? It is because of his impatience.

It came about long ago in the days when all birds were white and the time had come for them to receive their colors and the patterns of their feathers. Loon and Raven agreed that they would decorate each other.

Raven started first, tattooing Loon black, using ashes from a fire and its bill as a tattooing needle. Then he painted a beautiful white pattern over it like dazzling white stars against the night sky. Loon was pleased with Raven's tattooing and proud of its new plumage.

So now it was Loon's turn to tattoo Raven. Loon was a great artist and very patient in its work. It began to tattoo Raven with colors similar to its own, but Raven was impatient and became annoyed at Loon. Raven screamed and cried every time Loon's beak tattooed it. Then Raven cawed loudly, telling Loon to hurry up and finish its work.

Finally Raven became so impatient and tiresome that Loon gave up. Loon threw the ashes all over Raven and dove deep under the water to escape Raven's wrath.

To this day, Raven is all black.

LOON ASHAMED OF ITS FEATHERS

*A*nother story, told by the Hudson Bay Inuit, also tells of the plumage of the loon and the raven. But in this variation, the loon is so ashamed of its "comical" coloring that it becomes the source of the loon's shyness:

THE GREAT SPIRIT had two bird-children that he wished might resemble each other. He painted the first one, Loon, with a white breast and square spots on the back. The other bird-child, Raven, saw how comical Loon appeared, and laughed so much that Loon became ashamed and escaped to the water, where it always presents its white breast in order to hide the spots on its back that caused so much ridicule.

Common Loon Taking Flight

A loon dashes across Lake Gogebic in the upper peninsula of Michigan to gain flight. A legend from the Arikara people of the American prairies describes one benefit of the loon's difficult takeoff. Mother Corn was leading the people west to the land that was to become their home. Along the way they encountered many trials but overcame all—until they were confronted by a vast lake, too deep to cross and too wide to circle. Mother Corn and the people were about to abandon all hope when Loon appeared before them and promised to make a pathway through the water. Loon beat its wings and ran across the water, parting the waters of the lake like Moses had parted the Red Sea, and the people crossed safely to their promised land. (Photo © Dr. Scott Nielsen)

LOON WOMAN AND HER NECKLACE

There are several stories that tell how the loon got its distinctive necklace of white feathers. The Inuit tell the story of a blind boy whose sight is restored by a loon and who then gives the loon a necklace made of shells in thanks.

Another story, told by some of the Native American tribes of the Great Plains and recounted in several variations, tells the harrowing tale of Loon Woman and how the loon received its necklace:

A FAMILY HAD two children, a young girl and a young boy, but the boy was kept hidden away from the world and even his sister did not know of his existence.

One day, the sister, known as Loon Woman, found a single strand of hair in her family's home. The hair was spectacularly beautiful, unlike any hair she had ever before seen, and she pledged her undying love to the person to whom the hair belonged. Little did she know that hair belonged to her own blood brother.

Loon Woman became obsessed by love for the person whose hair she held, and when one day she discovered that the hair belonged to her secret brother, her love did not fade. She found this brother hidden by her parents and took him far away from her family so she could have him as her own.

Loon Woman confessed her love to her brother. The boy, believing her love to be devoted love between brother and sister, told her that he also loved her. But soon the boy realized that his sister desired him, and he cried out and ran away back to their family.

Loon Woman threatened to create a great fire that would destroy the family and all the world within it if the brother did not return to her. She vowed revenge and cried with great fury, but the family escaped to the sky, flying away in a large basket carried by a balloon, out of the reach of Loon Woman.

As the family flew away to safety, however, the boy made the mistake of looking down from the basket to earth, the fire, and his enraged sister. Suddenly the balloon burst and the family plummeted to earth, into the flames of the great fire. As they burned, their hearts burst forth from their bodies. Crying for her lost love, Loon Woman gathered up the heart of her beloved brother as well as of her parents and made a necklace from them, a necklace the loon wears to this day.

THE LOON IN FLIGHT

The loon's grace in flight is a sharp contrast to its ungainly takeoff and landing. Once in the air, loons have a distinctively aerodynamic profile that can be spotted from afar. But in attempting to take off, loons look almost is if they are drowning. They exert tremendous energy in their awkward sprints across the surface of the water, accentuated by the tapping of their webbed feet and wing tips slapping the water's surface. When alighting, they sometimes appear as though they are on the verge of a crash landing.

The loon's body has evolved for diving, and its solid rather than hollow bones and relatively short wingspan are ideal adaptations in aiding it to submerge and fish under water. Yet these same solid bones are part of the bird's overall heavy weight in comparison with other birds that have adapted primarily for flight.

Loons have the smallest wing surface in proportion to their weight of any flying bird. To make up for this, their wings have more curvature when distended for flying, which provides more lift than with some birds' wings. They also fly with a rapid wing beat for birds of their size, up to 250–270 beats per minute, or four wing beats per second.

Because of their small wing surface, loons require a long run on the surface of the water before they can take off. In fact, they are unable to rise from a solid surface, except for the smaller red-throated loon, which some observers claim to have seen take off from land.

But in flight, loons are graceful and powerful, and are able to fly long distances in search of food or during migration. Common loons have been clocked at up to 62 mph air speed (100 km/h), and there is an instance of a loon being chased by an airplane at speeds up to 80–100 mph (128–160 km/h).

The following excerpts are observations on the loons' beauty in flight—and comical labors to take off or land:

THE LOON NAVIGATES the air as a high powered cruiser plows the sea under forced draft. Perfection of design, with ample power effectively applied, produce the desired result. The lines are perfect; the strong neck and breast, terminating in the long sharp bill, are outstretched to pierce the air like the keenest spear; the heavy body, tapering fore and aft, glides through the air with the least possible resistance; and the big feet, held close together and straight out behind, form an effective rudder. The power is applied by wings—which seem too small—driven at high speed by large and powerful muscles. Its weight gives it stability and great momentum. It can not rise off the land at all and before it can rise from the water it must patter along the surface, half running and half flying, beating the water with both feet and wings, for a long distance; even then it experiences considerable difficulty unless facing a strong wind. But when once under way its flight is strong, direct, rapid, and long sustained.

—Arthur Cleveland Bent, *Life Histories of North American Diving Birds*, 1919

IT CANNOT FLY, but flutters along on the surface of the water, or dives for security when pursued.

—Meriwether Lewis, *History of the Expedition of Captains Lewis and Clark 1804-5-6*, 1905

STILL I HAD the pleasure at any rate, which I had not yet enjoyed, of seeing a heavy loon flying far above my head. Hitherto I had only seen the loon swim and dive, and almost doubted whether it could fly. In fact, flying causes it some difficulty; at least, rising in the air does. People say it requires wind for the purposes, and can hardly do it in calm weather. But, when once under way, it flies not only high but for a long distance, and makes great journeys both in spring and autumn. The loon we saw was quite alone, and soared like an eagle.

—Johann Georg Kohl, *Kitchi-Gami: Life Among the Lake Superior Ojibway*, 1860

IT IS SAID not to be able to take wing from the ground at all. In rising from the water the bird humps over in agony of effort, rising only by slow stages, first by threshing the surface of the water with wings and feet, then by combined running and flying, until the feet clear at last, and the aspirant at-

tains a proper motion. Once started, the loon's flight is swift and powerful, the wings accomplishing by rapid vibration what they lack in expanse. But the hapless act of the loon's life is that of alighting.

—W. L. Dawson, *The Birds of California*, 1923.

THE LOON ON LAND

*I*n their guide *Birds of the Soviet Union*, G. P. Dement'ev and N. A. Gladkov succinctly sum up the loon's plight when on land: "Terrestrially helpless." As with its efforts to take off for flight, the loon is hampered on land by the same features that make it such a fine diver. Its body has evolved for underwater swimming and its legs are positioned far back on its body where they serve the primary duty of propelling the loon after fish. This positioning of the legs makes for a wobbling walk that is almost painful to watch, as noted in the following observations of the loon on land:

THE LOON IS A very remarkable bird, from the formation of its feet. . . . They are so made, that it can scarcely walk; it is therefore seldom seen on land. In calm weather it rises from the water with great difficulty, and flies as impelled by the wind, on which it seems to depend.

—J. Long, *Voyages and Travels of an Indian Interpreter and Trader*, 1791

IN SINGULAR CONTRAST to the loon's facility and grace in the water is its behavior upon land. Since the feet are placed so far back, it must stand nearly upright, penguin-fashion; and its walk is an awkward, shuffling performance; or else, as is more likely to be the case, the bird flounders on all fours.

—W. L. Dawson, *The Birds of California*, 1923

NANEBOUJOU FORMS THE LOON

*T*he Anishinabeg people tell a story of the origins of the loon's odd-shaped body in a meandering, epic tale that bears resemblance to that of Jonah and the whale—and also explains several other animals' traits along the way.

In this legend, the loon's body was deformed by the

Anishinabeg hero Naneboujou, also known by various pronunciations, including Winabojo and Menaboju. Naneboujou is a whimsical, funny, and very human character, who is in some tales credited with creating the world, and at other times is a picaresque wanderer who often gets himself in trouble through his own devices. In this tale, Naneboujou has killed the largest fish in Lake Superior, the great Fish King. The story was recorded by German explorer Johann Georg Kohl in his *Kitchi-Gami: Life Among the Lake Superior Ojibway*, published in 1860:

NANEBOUJOU TIED THE Fish King behind his canoe and triumphantly paddled for home. He invited all the animals from the plains and the forests to a great feast to celebrate his feat, and they made merry.

The bear profited the most from this feast. He drank fish oil in tankards and grew so fat that he had to sleep for six months to lose weight. To this day, his body is layered with fat from this great meal.

But not all animals had such big paws to help themselves to the feast. The rabbit and the pheasant could only eat a few crumbs, and to this day they only have small amounts of fat on their bodies.

As host, Naneboujou regaled his guests, but before he himself had a chance to eat, all of the fish was consumed. Looking around the table at all his well-fed friends, however, gave him an idea, and he suggested a game of blindman's bluff. All the animals closed their eyes and danced around Naneboujou, who then had his pick of the fattest animals. He grabbed them by the neck and threw them into the kitchen, where his wife began cooking once again.

Naneboujou had put aside many good roasts for his dinner—and in fact for the whole of winter—when along came Loon, dancing with the others, eyes shut tight. Loon noticed that it was growing quieter at the feast, and so he opened one eye just in time to see Naneboujou strangle a fat goose.

Loon cried out a warning to the other remaining guests: "Oh, you animals! Naneboujou will kill us all!" All of the others opened their eyes and ran in terror.

Naneboujou was naturally beside himself with anger and chased after Loon. He caught Loon at the water's edge, but Loon was too fast and Naneboujou only had enough time to give Loon a well-placed kick. This wrathful kick displaced the entire body structure of Loon, robbed him of his tail, and moved his legs as far back as one sees them to this day. Since that time, Loon has become a shy bird and when he notices one of Naneboujou's relatives, he dives deep into the depths of the water.

Preening Loon
To preen, loons use their bills to squeeze oil from the uropygial gland located at the base of their tail. They grasp feathers in their bill and pull them through the bill to coat them in the rejuvenating oil. To reach the back of their head and neck, they rub the oil on their wings and then roll their head backwards. (Photo © Gregory M. Nelson)

Audubon Illustration of Red-Throated Loons

Above: *John James Audubon is the most famous American naturalist. He was born in 1785, in the West Indies, the son of a French naval officier and a Creole woman. An explorer, frontiersman, and ornithologist, he is best known today as an artist, due to his elegant and exacting color engravings of birds. These illustrations were collected in his grand tome,* The Birds of America, *first published by Audubon in London in 1827–1830. He illustrated the red-throated loon in various stages of its life and seasonal plumage.*

Aggression Dance

Facing page: *An adult common loon charges across the top of the water performing an aggression dance to scare off an intruding loon and protect its chicks. Loons often accompany this intense defense display with their tremolo call, a cry of warning or alarm. A variation of the Inuit story of how Loon and Raven tattooed each other to color their plumage tells that Raven laughed at Loon's comical appearance. Loon was ashamed, and henceforth he always shows his bare, white breast in this dance to hide the spots on his back from the world.* (Photo © Gregory M. Nelson)

LOVE AMONG THE LOONS

*L*oons are great exhibitionists during the breeding season. Driven by sexual excitement, both males and females perform a series of curious courtship antics. Ornithologist Thomas S. Roberts described the courtship of a pair of loons in his classic book *The Birds of Minnesota*:

THE COURTSHIP OF a pair of Loons, which may be witnessed in the early spring before they leave the open lakes, is an interesting and engaging performance. On one of the park lakes of Minneapolis, on April 8, 1925, a pair thus engaged was watched for some time at close range by the writer and a group of students. The birds approached one another slowly from a distance of several feet, ducking their heads at short intervals, usually beneath the surface of the water, and making two or three such "bows" before they came together. When they met they put their heads near together for just an instant and then quickly dove, one directly under the other, coming up almost at once several feet apart, and, turning about, began the performance all over again. Finally one bird, presumably the male, seemed to become more excited, standing up on the water and flapping its wings rapidly, following which it began scooting quickly back and forth over the surface with body flat and wings extended, propelling itself by its feet. When this began, the other bird grew indifferent and paddled slowly out into the lake, leaving the male to "carry on" alone, a performance that did not last long.

Ornithologist J. S. Huxley similarly studied red-throated loons in Spitsbergen, Norway. He named one courtship display the "Snake Ceremony" for the shape the loons make of their bodies during the demonstration: "Two birds swim, one behind the other, having necks arched with snake-like effect and bill wide open but tips submerged; bodies in normal position and the motion not violent."

Huxley named another display the "Plesiosaur Race," again due to the loons' odd body posture, which made them look like the *Plesiosaurus* dinosaur. This courtship display was often accompanied by a special growl as well as splashing and diving:

Usually two or three birds take part in it, sometimes four. The birds depressed the hinder half of the body below the water: body held at an angle so that the breast and shoulders were stuck out: neck upwards and forwards in a stiff position: head and beak inclined somewhat forward, again rather stiffly. Thus the birds swam through the water, accompanying one another. They would go for some distance in this way, then would turn and continue the process in the opposite direction. Usual arrangement is for one bird to lead, the other two being half a length or less behind.

LOONS IN LOVE

*J*ohn James Audubon waxed poetic on the wooing of two red-throated loons in *The Birds of America*:

HIGH OVER THESE waters, the produce of the melted snows, the red-throated diver is seen gamboling by the side of his mate. The males emit their love notes, and, with neck gracefully curved downward, speed by the females, saluting them with mellow tones as they pass. In broad circles they wheel their giddy flight, and now, with fantastic gliding and curves, they dive toward the spot of their choice. Alighted on the water, how gracefully they swim, how sportively they beat it with their strong pinions, how quickly they plunge and rise again, and how joyously do they manifest to each other the depth and intensity of their affection.

Courtship Dance
A pair of red-throated loons dance together across a Swedish lake in an elaborate courtship ritual. Driven by sexual excitement, all loons are great exhibitionists during the breeding season, but the red-throated loon is perhaps the most overt and demonstrative. Ornithologist J. S. Huxley named the display shown here the "Plesiosaur Race" due to the odd body posture of the red-throated loons, which he likened to a Plesiosaurus *dinosaur.* (Photo © Janos Jurka [Bruce Coleman Ltd.])

The Diver

I am the sovereign of the sea,
A king in the kingdom of the waves.
—From "The Story of the Loon"
in Johann Georg Kohl's
Kitchi-Gami: Life Among the Lake
Superior Ojibway, **1860**

Over the last ten million years, loons have evolved into highly specialized birds ideally suited for swimming and diving. Among other anatomical and physiological attributes, their bodies are streamlined to help them cut through water, and their bones are solid, so they are less buoyant. As author Candace Savage wrote in her *Wings of the North*, "Common Loons might be thought of as seals with wings, so thoroughly are they adapted to an aquatic life." In fact, a legend from Finland tells that the loon was first created without legs, but nature, becoming sensible of its mistake, flung a pair of legs after it.

Yet even today, when we know much more about the loon's adaptation for diving, the bird still retains an element of mystery when it dives. In the British Isles, the loon is sometimes known as the Hell-diver, a bird that dove to the depths of the world's waters. Native American stories tell of the loon diving to the spirit world beneath the water to visit the souls of deceased ancestors.

Common Loons at Sunrise
A family of common loons swims among lily pads as the sun rises through the morning fog. Loons evolved to become expert swimmers and divers with streamlined bodies, solid bones that are less bouyant, and powerful, rear-mounted legs that are ideal for propelling them through the water. (Photo © Gregory M. Nelson)

On another note, the loon in Medieval Europe symbolized people who were preoccupied with sex, as the loon was so fond of diving under water.

THE GREAT DIVER

Known fittingly as the "diver" in the British Isles, the loon's greatest talent is in diving and swimming under water in search of fish and other food. Loons have a number of different types of dives for feeding, as well as sinking, jerking, or sliding under the water.

Much of the bird's anatomical evolution and adapted behavior has been shaped by its diving. Eldon Greij, publisher and editor of *Birder's World* magazine, recently detailed a typical dive and the anatomy and physiology that make the loon's underwater swimming possible:

LOONS ARE SUPERBLY adapted for swimming and diving. Loons are known to dive as deep as 180 feet and the longest recorded dive is 15 minutes, but most are much shorter. A number of anatomical and physiological adaptations makes this possible.

Their wings are reduced in size, all the better for diving. Legs are positioned far back on the body and extend laterally like oars when swimming. This allows easy steering and maximum thrust without interference from turbulence created by the other foot, as would occur if the legs were close together. Unlike other birds, the lower leg of loons has an elongate process (cnemial crest) that extends prominently above the knee. This crest increases the surface area for attachment of the large thigh muscles, thereby giving loons powerful leg extension. The large webbed foot generates much force against the water. When bringing the foot forward in the recovery stroke, the web is collapsed, which, when combined with the flattened tarsus, minimizes resistance to the water.

Before diving, loons, arch their bodies and rise slightly from the water, then gracefully slice through the surface. Just prior to the dive, the body is compressed, forcing out air and making the bird less buoyant. Unlike most birds, which have hollow bones, loons have heavy, marrow-filled bones that increase their specific gravity, making it easier to swim under water.

Diving birds store higher amounts of oxygen in their blood and muscle than non-divers. Normally, oxygen is used in metabolism, but under extreme conditions, such as diving, metabolism in some parts of the body must be carried out anaerobically (without oxygen). The heart and central nervous system, however, must have oxygen at all times. Immediately upon immersion, therefore, a diving reflex lowers the heart rate by about half, which reduces the rate at which the heart utilizes oxygen. As a further aid, blood flow is redirected from the skin and muscle to the heart and central nervous system, ensuring that they get the oxygen needed.

When the diving reflex kicks in, muscle and most other tissues switch to anaerobic metabolism. Besides conserving oxygen, this process also reduces the output of carbon dioxide, another distinct advantage because carbon dioxide build-up forces an animal to breathe, something divers want to avoid. Additionally, in divers, the breathing center of the brain has a high tolerance for carbon dioxide, which helps delay the initiation of the next breath.

There is a price to pay for some adaptations. The small wings [in relation to the loon's heavy weight] make for laborious flight and require a running start on the water to become airborne. Furthermore, the placement of the legs far back on the body makes loons nearly helpless on land. But the advantages far outweigh the disadvantages.

"CAUSING CONSTERNATION AMONG THE FINNY TRIBES"

The diving exploits of the loon are the stuff of legend. Ornithologists, writers, and the just plain curious throughout history have mused on the underwater exploits of this

Loon in Fog
An adult common loon surfaces from a dive and vigorously flaps its wings to shake excess water from the feathers and shuffle them back into place. Loons reportedly can dive to two hundred feet (60 meters) below the surface and have been caught in deepwater fishing nets. When frightened or pursued by an enemy, they may stay submerged for up to three minutes. Typically, however, they dive for food at much shallower depths and stay submerged no more than sixty seconds. (Photo © Bruce Montagne)

prodigious diving bird. After marveling on the loon's prowess, Charlton Ogburn mused in *The Adventure of Birds* that "no one knows how deep some of the aquatic birds may dive, or could with strong incentive." The following excerpts are further observations on the diving ability of the loon:

THE LOON IS a rapid swimmer and a wonderful diver. It is much more at home in the water than elsewhere. Its plunge beneath the surface is exceedingly quick and graceful, causing little disturbance; with wings closely folded, it is propelled by its powerful paddles alone, which usually work alternately, driving it at a high speed. The loon can swim for a long distance under water and always prefers to escape in this way.
—Arthur Cleveland Bent, *Life Histories of North American Diving Birds*, 1919

THE DIVING POWERS of this species are remarkable, and also its speed under water; I have seen it traverse what I feel certain was fully half a mile below the surface, in an incredibly short space of time.
—Henry H. Slater, *Manual of the Birds of Iceland*, 1901

THIS LOON FEEDS largely on fish, which it pursues beneath the surface with wonderful power and speed. The subaqueous rush of this formidable monster must cause great consternation among the finny tribes. Even a party of fish-hunting mergansers is promptly scattered before the onslaught of such a powerful rival; they recognize his superior strength

Adult Loon Feeding Chick
Surfacing from a dive for food, an adult common loon feeds a minnow to a one-week-old chick riding on the back of another adult. Loons feed on freshwater fish such as minnows, suckers, perch, sunfish, smelt, and trout; and saltwater fish such as herring, sea trout, and flounder. They also feed on crayfish, crab, shrimp, leeches, frogs, salamanders, and aquatic insects.
(Photo © Gregory M. Nelson)

45

Calling Chick
A chick tries out its fledgling call while perched safely atop its parent's back. Loons often carry their young on their backs to protect them and allow them to rest while they learn to swim. (Photo © W. E. Ruth, Tom Walker—Agent)

Hiding Posture
With a bald eagle soaring overhead, a common loon rides low in the water in a hiding posture. Already partially submerged, the loon is prepared to dive in an instant if provoked. Loons dive from the surface with a simple forward thrust of the body, a movement that can seem almost instantaneous if you blink while watching a swimming bird. (Photo © Bill Kinney)

and speed, as he plunges in among them, and must stand aside until his wants are satisfied. Even the lively trout, noted for its quickness of movement, cannot escape the loon and large numbers of these desirable fish are destroyed to satisfy its hunger. Some sportsmen have advocated placing a bounty on loons on this account, but as both loon and trout have always flourished together until the advent of the sportsmen, it is hardly fair to blame this bird, which is such an attractive feature of the wilds, for the scarcity of the trout. We are too apt to condemn a bird for what little damage it does in this way, without giving it credit for the right to live.

—Arthur Cleveland Bent, *Life Histories of North American Diving Birds*, 1919

IT SWIMS RAPIDLY on the surface or with its body submerged. In diving it can sink quietly out of sight or dive like a flash, causing scarcely a ripple; but when not hurried or when intending to make a deep dive the neck is arched and the body thrown forward in a downward plunge with the wings closely pressed to the sides. Under water it makes astonishing speed, faster than a man can run along the shore, and it is useless to pursue one in a boat or a canoe; it can even outdistance an ordinary power boat. I believe that it ordinarily swims under water by using its feet alone, working them alternately; but when an extra burst of speed is desired the wings are also brought into play and the result is marvelous.

—Arthur Cleveland Bent, *Life Histories of North American Diving Birds*, 1919

THE LOON AS TALISMAN

Due to the loon's wizardry in catching fish, the bird, throughout much of its range, became a symbol of success in the field for hunters and anglers. On Puget Sound, the Puyallup people, who knew the loon as *Swoxqwad,* revered it as a powerful fisher; the symbol of the *Swoxqwad* on a boat or hat lent a person the force to be a good hunter or fisher.

The loon was also used as a talisman by the Inuit, who sometimes painted the master fisher on their kayaks. Edward S. Curtis, author of *The North American Indian,* described how some of the Inuit hunters kept a carving of their talisman with them in their kayaks and handed down the talisman

through the generations:

THE BELIEF IS that the spirit-power of the animal will become embodied in the kaiak and aid materially in catching game. The original talismans may be the shaved noses of land animals, such as bear, mink, or fox; or birds, or sea animals, and are often objects carved from ivory or wood. These are kept in a wrapping of bark inside of a parchment roll of hair-seal bladder and are taken from their coverings only during the Bladder feast, when they are worn on headgear. When a man dies, his talismans are all wound in one bundle and given to the surviving sons; or, failing sons, are divided amongst the nearest relatives. Usually some particular talisman is handed down in a family from father to son.

The possessor of a talisman acquires supernatural power through the spirit of the animal, bird, or fish which it represents. A man's mark on kaiak, masks, weapons, or walrus- and seal-skins, is a medium through which the spirit-power always keeps in touch with the owner. It is also a mark of identification. It is taboo for a man to eat, wear, or even touch the animal, bird, or fish which his talisman represents, for his spirit would then be destroyed.

THE RED EYE OF THE LOON

The loon's ruby red eyes are perhaps its most fascinating features. In addition to the call of the loon, the intense, scarlet eyes create a mysterious aura and a prehistoric, otherworldly look. All five loon species have red eyes.

In natural light, the loon's eyes appear red because they reflect red light. But water filters out most red light, and so when hunting underwater, the loon's eyes appear black and thus invisible to their prey. Some researchers also believe the red eyes may allow the loon to see better in the filtered light under water. But many questions about the loon's red eyes remain unanswered, and these theories are not universally accepted by the scientific community.

In addition, loons have a third eyelid, known as a nictitating membrane. This eyelid, common to many birds and reptiles, not only keeps the eye clean by blinking, but is also transparent and, for the loon, works as a sort of lens to aid underwater vision by increasing the eye's refractive power.

The Red-Eyed Loon
The eyes of all five species of loons glow a deep red. The eerie red color naturally became the impetus for legends and superstitions the world over. According to loon researcher Judith W. McIntyre, early graves uncovered in Alaska contained corpses with artificial eyes placed in their sockets; a loon buried nearby had been prepared similarly, suggesting that the loon could see beyond this world and accompany the dead to the spirit kingdom. (Photo © Gregory M. Nelson)

THE LOON AND THE BLIND BOY

A story told by the Inuit of Alaska is an enchanting link between the loon's diving expertise and an ages-old belief in the bird's ability to restore sight to the blind. The story of "The Loon and the Blind Boy" is an eerie connection to the bird's own red eyes. This legend has been recounted many times by different storytellers and is paraphrased here from a variety of sources.

LONG AGO, A blind boy lived along the ocean with his ancient grandmother in a house made of whale bones and stones covered by animal skins. The boy had been blind since birth, and thus he could not hunt or fish although he deeply desired to do so to prove his worth by providing food. Instead, he spent his days sitting alone along the shores of the waters playing with a simple necklace made of shells, which was his sole worldly possession and had been given to him by his true mother before she died.

Unbeknownst to the blind boy, his grandmother was in truth an evil witch doctor. One day in a fit of rage, she told the blind boy that he was worthless as he could neither hunt nor fish. She cast him out of the house, saying, "Do not return until you can bring food for us to live on." She told him to go to the ocean and make a snare trap to catch a loon for their dinner.

The blind boy did as he was told, using driftwood and strips of dried animal ligaments to fashion a snare along the water's edge. Then he hid behind a large rock and waited soundlessly for a loon to approach.

The blind boy hid behind the rock, feeling the cold of the day and his hunger in his stomach. Finally, he heard a great splashing of water and flapping of wings followed by silence—broken by the sad cry of a loon caught in his trap. The blind boy rushed forth from his hiding place to triumphantly take the loon home to his grandmother for dinner.

But as he picked up the loon he felt a single tear fall from the bird into his hand, and the blind boy too felt sadness at the loon's capture. Then the blind boy received another surprise: the loon spoke to him, saying, "Please don't kill me, blind boy, as I too have a family to provide for. Instead, let me help you."

The loon told the blind boy that he would restore the boy's sight. The blind boy must dive into the water with the loon and the water would bring back the use of the boy's eyes.

So the boy freed the loon and climbed on his back.

Komokwa Mask With Loon Guardian
Loons were regarded with reverence by the Kwakwaka'wakw people of British Columbia. This mask depicts the face of Komokwa, King of the Undersea World, Master and Protector of Seals. Komokwa ruled the seas from a grand, underwater palace built of fabulous copper, and his kingdom was guarded by loons and served by seals. As diving birds, loons belonged both to the air and the surface world as well as to the underwater realm where the spirits of the dead dwelt; loons could travel freely between the two worlds, and thus were held in awe and wonder. The mask is made of painted wood, cloth, and bits of mirror; the loon guardian on top of Komokwa's head has moveable canvas wings controlled by pieces of twine. The mask was crafted by Charlie George, Sr., of the 'Mimkwlis band in the early twentieth century, and measures twenty-two inches (55 cm) in height. (Courtesy of the Museum of Anthropology, University of British Columbia, Vancouver, Canada, Catalog #A3588)

Together they dove into the icy cold water of the ocean, the blind boy clinging to the feathers of the loon. They dove deep down into the water until the boy feared his lungs were going to burst. Then they surfaced, and the blind boy could make out the difference between light and dark, shadow and sun.

The loon dove again with the boy still on its back, and this time when they surfaced, the boy could see objects clearly. He could make out the rock he had hid behind and the snare trap he had made.

The loon dove a final time, swimming to the bottom of the lake, keeping the boy under water so long he thought he would never come up again. Yet when the loon brought the boy to the surface, the boy could see perfectly—and he could see in other ways as well. He saw that his grandmother was a witch and that it was she who had made him blind and killed his mother.

The boy turned to the loon and thanked the bird for its gift. The boy then made a gift to the loon of the shell necklace that his own mother had given him, hanging the necklace around the loon's throat for all the world and all the ages to see.

The boy returned home empty-handed and his evil grandmother shrieked at him, "Where is the food I sent you to find?" But the boy cast the crone out of the house and made the door fast. Throughout the cold of the night, he heard her calling for him, first in anger, then in kindness, a spell to lure him to open the door for her. By morning she had frozen, and the boy opened the door to see her body lying there. From a rock near the water, he saw a large owl, which he could see was his grandmother's evil spirit. The owl-woman hooted at him in anger and desperation, and then flew away forever.

Common Loon in Fog

An adult common loon sails through the morning fog hovering above a lake. Glooscap, the legendary Algonquin hero who taught Loon its call, also taught Loon a valuable lesson. One day Loon went diving for food and got stuck in the weeds at the bottom of the lake. Loon cried out, but Glooscap could not hear him. Then the sky began to thunder, telling Glooscap that Loon was in trouble. Glooscap dove to the depths of the lake to free Loon just before he drowned. When Loon recovered, Glooscap told him he must never dive into the weeds. Even today, the loon remembers this lesson.
(Photo © Stephen Kirkpatrick)

The Call of the Loon

More than any other feature, the loon's incantatory call has captured the hearts and imaginations of people from time immemorial. It echoes through ancient Native American creation legends and Siberian folktales. Even today, in this age of modernism, the lonely call of the loon calms the mind and soothes the soul.

Yet this call and its power are impossible to truly describe in words—although many have tried. Early explorers and latter-day ornithologists alike have attempted to evoke, examine, and explain the call's allure. But perhaps American poet Robert Bly came closest in his poem "The Loon's Cry" in which he writes, "It was the cry of someone who owned very little."

And still there's more to it, an even greater significance in this cry. The call has been compared to a baby's wailing, the scream of a lunatic, hellish hysteria—or to a peal of ecstatic laughter triggered by the joy of simply being alive.

Even the shores seemed hushed and waiting for that first lone call, and when it came, a single long-drawn mournful noise, the quiet was deeper than before.
—**Sigurd F. Olson**, *Listening Point*

The Song of the Wild
A Native American legend explains how the loon got its cry—or rather, lost its talking voice. One day, Loon and Crow were fishing together but Loon was catching all the fish. In a fit of rage, Crow cut out Loon's tongue and threw him in the water. To this day, the loon can no longer speak but can only call out a lonely cry. (Photo © Woody Hagge)

THE SOUND OF THE BEGINNING OF TIME

The first act in the creation of the world, according to an Anishinabeg legend, was the solitary voice of the Spirit-Creator calling out across the primordial void, reverberating through the emptiness to become embodied in the great cry of the loon.

The Sun then rose out of the total darkness, and the first light of the first day distinguished itself from the depth of the black shadows, and the light too became embodied in the black and white plumage of the loon.

Thus the loon was not only present at the beginning of all things, but it was the creation.

THE LOON'S VOCAL COMMUNICATION

Loon researcher Judith W. McIntyre has spent more than twenty years studying the common loon throughout North America, from its summer nesting habitat in Canada to its wintering grounds in Virginia. A professor of biology at Utica College of Syracuse University, she is vice president of the North American Loon Fund and organized the first public survey of loon populations in the U.S., Minnesota's Project Loon Watch, in 1971. In her essential study, *The Common Loon: Spirit of Northern Lakes*, she details the four primary types of the loon's vocal communication:

Loons calls are distinctive, exciting, easily heard and recognized, and are given throughout most of the spring and summer. Loons use a variety of calls, which can be placed in one of four categories: hoots, wails, tremolos, and yodels. Some are soft and carry for only a short distance. Others travel over the lakes for tremendous distances. These calls have become the symbol of wilderness, the positive affirmation of wild places, wild things, and wild sounds in the night.

Hoots are short, single notes given among individuals in close proximity to one another. They are a form of contact call because they permit individuals to keep in touch with each other. Loons hoot during ritualized social gatherings and on the fall staging grounds. Hoots are also used by one loon as it approaches a group or enters the territory of another loon.

Wails are unmodulated pure tones, and may be given as one-note, two-note, or three-note calls. One-note wails consist of a single unbroken note, two-note wails begin on the same note but move quickly to a second note of higher frequency, and three-note wails add a third and higher frequency component to the two-note version. The note of highest frequency is held the longest, about two seconds, in all versions, although it can continue for as long as three seconds or be abbreviated to a single second.

One-note wails are a single note, but the frequency gradually increases to the middle of the call, and then just as gradually returns to its original pitch. There is not a break between one frequency and a shift to a higher or lower one.

Two-note wails have a first note like the one-note version, but it is shorter, and the second note is longer and at a higher frequency. In musical terms, there is commonly a major fourth between the first and second notes, although the exact interval may vary among individuals. As an example, if the first note is G in the second octave above middle C, the second note goes up to higher C. The call may end on the higher note, or it may return to the original. The average length of the call is two seconds, but this is far from uniform, and as with the one-note call, there are short two-note wails, as well as those which continue for nearly three seconds.

The first two notes of three-note wails are the same as the two-note version, and the third rises to a still higher pitch, usually an interval of a diminished fifth. For example, if the

Sound of the Wilderness
The call of the loon is echoed in superstitions around the world. From Norway to Iceland, people believe the call foretells rain. In the Faeroe Islands, if a loon gives its call during a funeral, it is a sign that the loon is helping the deceased soul in its passage to heaven. A Norwegian folk saying holds that a loon's call prophesizes that someone will drown. (Photo © Gregory M. Nelson)

two-note wail just described begins the call, the third note rises to F# so there is nearly a complete octave between the first and third notes, or almost a doubling of the frequency. There may be a return to the second note at the end of the call, or the wail may end on the highest frequency.

Family members use several versions of wail calls. These are the "family wails." There is a soft one-note wail given between pair members, the "mew" or "ma" call. It is deliberate and soft, and rises to a perceptibly higher frequency in the middle than do other one-note wails, then falls to the lower pitch at the end. Its duration is one second.

Wails serve as mechanisms to reduce distance between loons. Loons move toward each other when they are wailing, and if one loon wails, its mate approaches, and may also begin to wail. Wails indicate a desire for closer contact, and the more intense the wail, the greater the urgency for contact and assistance. Wails develop from chick distress calls as there is a similarity in call types, including a change from a one-note to a two-note and finally to a three-note as the level of frustration increases. This happens with chicks, but because during adult calling the responding individual also wails its answer, I wonder if wails would better be interpreted as indicating a willingness to interact, with all the range of messages and meanings that that definition could imply.

Parents use wails to call chicks off the nest, to signal when they have food for them, and to retrieve them from their hiding places. Males use the soft version to lure females ashore for copulation, pair members use it with each other when they are separated, and it is given by both pair members when they approach each other. Wails seem to be the loon versions of "come here" and "here I come."

When pair members wail at each other they usually begin with a one-note call, then go to a two-note version, and may

Yellow-Billed Loon's Warning Cry
Backlit by the morning sun shining through fog, a yellow-billed loon calls out from its nest along Alaska's Colville River delta leading to the Arctic Ocean. The loon's call has been described differently by almost every listener: naturalist Sigurd Olson tagged it a "wild, rollicking laughter," while John McPhee labeled it the eerie "laugh of the deeply insane." (Photo © Gary Schultz)

continue to a three-note wail if the mate does not respond. I have often wondered if wails that initiate nocturnal choruses might be given as a loon seeks its mate. Perhaps sleeping loons tend to drift apart, and from time to time awaken and vocally search for each other.

Tremolos, or laughing calls, have been studied and described by W. E. Barklow. He recorded and analyzed nearly 3,000 tremolo calls from loons in northern Maine. He described tremolos as frequency-modulated calls of variable length, lasting from 0.15 to more than one second, and including between 1.5 and seven modulations, a modulation being one rise and fall in pitch.

Males call at a lower frequency than their mates do. If the pitch of a call is a reflection of body size, then, since males are larger than their mates, it would be expected that their voices would also be lower.

Barklow describes tremolos as alarm calls, given during threatening situations. This means it is often given when people approach a nest or chicks. It is no wonder tremolos are more often identified as "loon" than other calls are; people frequently, albeit unintentionally, intrude on loon family life.

Barklow noted a tendency to flee that accompanied the tremolo; the higher the frequency the greater the chance the bird would leave. Loons seem more reluctant to attack as frequency increases.

Some versions of the tremolo are given special names to indicate their special status. *Flight calls* are tremolos given by loons when they are flying. They are short, of constant length, with four to five modulations, and I believe they are timed to coincide with the flapping rate of flying loons. There are four flaps per call segment, and this may be linked to inhalation and exhalation, although the respiratory rate for loons in flight has not been confirmed. Flight calls are given by loons over occupied territories. They may or may not be answered by the territorial birds. Barklow also found that flight calls were primarily given over occupied territories; if loons flew over unclaimed lakes, they rarely gave a flight call.

Duets are antiphonal tremolos given by pair members. During calling, pair members alternate their signals, each given in different frequencies from that of its mate. Barklow found that pair members frequently used different call types, and this, too, would serve to exaggerate or maximize the pitch differences between the two birds.

Pairs use duets during nocturnal chorusing when it is difficult for observers to ascertain the exact context in which they are given. The loons are always too far away to see using any form of night scope I have tried. Nocturnal choruses include yodels as well as wails and tremolos.

Yodels, discussed below, are individually recognizable calls, and are given at night together or alternating with duets by members of a pair other than the yodeling bird. They emanate from territorial boundaries, suggesting that they are used to defend territories. Does the use of duets together with yodels suggest that duets are also used in territorial defense or proclamation? Duets are not thought to be used in loon pair bonding, as they are for several other species of birds.

Duets are also used in flight, especially when loons leave their territories during conflict situations. As a pair takes flight, it circles its territory, duetting as it goes. Surely there is an agonistic element in this behavior—components of both fear and defense are apparent. Nevertheless, I think it is safe to say a duet is a territorial statement.

Tremoloing birds are defensive, yet also have a tendency to flee. During high-intensity calling, loons run across the water, alternately approaching and retreating. Flight calls are given by birds passing over a territory, not by those landing. Birds leaving interactions on lakes other than their own give tremolos as they move away. A loon being chased is much more likely to tremolo than is the loon doing the chasing. Finally, a loon tremolos while defending its young from human intruders, runs across the water toward the disturbance, then turns and just as quickly runs the other way, or dives and comes up at a distance. These examples strongly suggest that tremolos are agonistic calls.

Yodels are male calls, perhaps the counterpart to male song in most other bird species. They seem to remain identical from year to year for any one loon, but so far no one has marked loons with colored wing tags or leg bands and then recorded their yodels from one year to the next. Since marked and banded loons return over and over to the same territory and individuals occupying the same territory also have the same yodel from one year to the next, it is highly probable that yodels are providing information on individual identity for other loons just as they are for biologists.

Warning Cry

A pair of common loons swims through a foggy sunrise, the lead bird calling to fend off an approaching loon. A Native American legend from the Pacific Northwest tells of the source of the loon's warning cry. A young boy went one day to a lake that his mother had warned him was haunted. But it was a nice day, and the boy could see no evil spirits in the lake, so he dove in. As the boy swam, he saw a fat trout swimming about; he caught the trout, brought it to shore, and cooked it. But the trout was a demon in disguise, and as the boy swallowed the last bite, he was changed into a loon. He flew home to his mother and called for her, but she could not understand him. To this day, loons cry to boys and girls, warning them to never disobey their mothers. (Photo © Gregory M. Nelson)

TIME SUSPENDED

The loon is an ancient creature, with its origins dating back millions of years—to the creation of life on Earth according to some stories. On certain nights in the wilderness, the loon's voice can evoke a sudden, intense illusion of timelessness or *déjà vu*, transporting the listener back through the ages.

Traveling through the Pacific Northwest in the early 1800s, explorer Thomas J. Farnham found himself one night at a strange place where time seemed suspended, a mood brought on in part by the call of the loon. He recounted that night along the Columbia River, in what is now the state of Washington, in his journal, *Travels in the Great Western Prairies*, published in 1843:

THE STARS WERE out on the clear night, twinkling as of old, when the lofty peaks around were heaved from the depths of the volcano. They now looked down on a less grand, indeed, but more lovely scene. The fires of the natives blazed among the woody glens, the light canoe skimmed the water near the shore, the winds groaned over the mountain tops, the cascades sang from cliff to cliff, the loon shouted and dove beneath the shining wave; it was a wild, almost unearthly scene. . . .

Some one hundred and fifty years later, naturalist writer Paul Gruchow found himself at a similar intersection of time and place. He recounted the evening in his essays on the Boundary Waters Canoe Area of Minnesota and Quetico Provincial Park of Ontario, *Travels in Canoe Country*:

DOWN THE LAKE a solitary loon cries. The sound is low and mournful. It is sometimes mistaken for the howl of a wolf. I think that the cry might have come from my own heart. When it echoes back across the water, it also echoes inside me, and the reverberations do not die away. I shiver, and button my wool shirt, and pull a jacket over it, but I think it is not the sudden coldness alone that stirs within me. . . . Nine thousand years ago, this lake was here. Eight thousand years ago, on a night very like this one, perhaps, an ancestor of mine sat upon this boulder, or on one nearby. A loon was crying, and its cry echoed across these waters, and the echo reverberated in my kin's heart, and it reverberates still.

Anishinabeg Courting Flute
Courting flutes were carved by the men of many Native American tribes to charm their beloved with music. As folklorist Frances Densmore wrote of the Anishinabeg flute players in her Chippewa Customs *of 1929, "The flute was played by the men to attract and please young maidens." Speaking of the flute's legendary creation in* American Indian Myths and Legends, *Henry Crow Dog of the Brule Sioux told Richard Erdoes, "That flute of ours, the siyotanka, is for only one kind of music—love music." This courting flute bears the likeness of a loon's head, symbolic of the loonlike sounds the flute could make in the hands of a skilled musician or love-stricken suitor. This flute was crafted by Minnesota Anishinabeg artist Jeffrey Chapman.* (Courtesy of the Science Museum of Minnesota)

60

DEFYING DESCRIPTION

British nature photographer G. K. Yeates attempts to describe the loon's cry in his book on Iceland, *The Land of the Loon*, but admits defeat. Instead, he chronicles several of the numerous similes that have been used down through time to convey the feel of the call. The British call the common loon the great northern diver:

THESE CACOPHONOUS DUETS and devilish calls of the great northern divers defy description. They have been described as hair-raising, and no one who has heard them would ever dispute the appropriateness of the description. It is only necessary to review the various similes which have been made to liken the calls of the diver family to realize how impossible it is to set such sounds to syllables: "the scream of a child in great pain"; "the barking of a small dog"; "a blood-curdling scream"; "a loud yelling"; "a rolling-growl". In short, if you imagine all the maniacs in hell catching hysteria at the same moment, you will get as clear a picture as any bewildered naturalist who has heard the real thing can hope to convey.

A CALL OF ANGUISH AND TRIUMPH

The effect of the loon's call is simply "devastating," according to naturalist writer Charlton Ogburn. He writes of the loon's magnificent voice in his *tour de force* on birds through the seasons, *The Adventure of Birds*:

THE LOON IS neither musician nor instrumentalist. It is a voice. From the forbidding waters off the coast it comes in May to northern lakes. There at evening in the dark reflection of the jagged forest, drawing behind it a V of waves that show as colored streamers of the sunset sky, it raises a cry that wells up out of the quiet in a clear falsetto and falls off to drift away into space:

"Ooo aaaaaaaaah oo." . . .

To drift away into space and into silence, a silence profound and intense. God only knows what you would think if you did not know the origin of that voice. You wait, nerves drawn.

"Oo ah eeeeeee ah oo."

The cry breaks upward for the "eeeeeee," abruptly descends to the "ah oo." The effect is devastating.

"Oo ah eeeeeee ah oo.

"Oo ah eeeeeee ah oo."

Other cries come from that half-human throat and another Loon or two across the water take them up: whinnies, softly fluttering and quavering—spectral voices calling up spirits—and a prolonged "Ooooooooo-ah" rising with what in a human being would be hysteria, to a "We-ah we-ah we-ah we-ah" such as you hear from gulls, breaking downward between the syllables. . . . And indeed, with Loons sounding from two or three quarters, each in the voice of two or three different beings, you could imagine yourself at a witches' Sabbath, a Walpurgis Night of the wilderness. But to me that broken, pealing cry is at once one of anguish and triumph such as life has surely earned the right to voice to the heavenly orbs as they come twinkling on.

THE CALL OF THE WILD

Many writers have described the allure of the loon's call, from the prolific American ornithologist Arthur Cleveland Bent, who favored poeticizing the lives of birds, to naturalist writer Sigurd F. Olson. To each scribe the call has a different meaning, but perhaps their writings are all simply attempts to describe the same, indescribable allure.

AMONG THE PICTURESQUE lakes of the wilder, wooded portions of the Northern States and Canada—where dark firs and spruces mingled with graceful white birches, cast their reflections in the still, clear waters—sportsmen and appreciative nature lovers have found attractive summer resorts. Here, far from the cares of the busy world, one finds true recreation in his pursuit of speckled trout, real rest in his camp among the fragrant balsams, and genuine joy in his communion with nature in her wildest solitudes. The woodland lakes would be solitudes, indeed, did they lack the finishing touch to make the picture complete, the tinge of wildness which adds color to the scene, the weird and mournful cry of the loon, as he calls to his mate or greets some new arrival. Who has ever paddled a canoe, or cast a fly, or pitched a tent in the north woods and has not stopped to listen to this wail of the wilderness? And what would the wilderness be without it?

—Arthur Cleveland Bent, *Life Histories of North American Diving Birds*, 1919

THEIR CRY IS loud, has a peculiarly low and melancholy tone, and, when often repeated, is said to portend rain. The Canadian voyagers never fail to make a loud hooting noise when this bird passes, for the purpose of rendering it, as they say, foolish.

—Alexander Wilson and Charles Lucian Bonaparte, *American Ornithology*, 1831

OFTEN TOWARD NIGHTFALL I have heard his wild storm-call far out to windward against the black pall of an approaching tempest like the howl of a lone wolf coming down the wind.

—Edward Howe Forbush, *The Natural History of the Birds of Eastern and Central North America*, 1939

LOONS ADD ENORMOUSLY to the fascination of the northern summer nights. When the air is perfectly still, when not a leaf moves and the midnight sun throws a red glare round the sky, tinging the glassy surface of the calm lakes, the loons start their weird, wild crying. The Indians say that they are calling for wind, without which they cannot fly; it is a peaceful and not unmusical sound, associated with the light summer nights by every one who knows the northern waterways.

—Michael H. Mason, *The Arctic Forests*, 1924

IN THE EARLY morning, the loon often rises from the water and flies in great sweeping circles, crying out an awakening morning bugle in harsh but resonant syllables. This chore of combined morning exercises and countryside rousing completed, the great diver glides back to the water and starts getting breakfast, stopping now and then to give way to great peals of laughter at the excellence of the food, the joy of being alive, or perchance at having awakened all the furred and feathered folks, as well as any stray men, with his greeting to the rising sun.

—Ira N. Gabrielson and Frederick C. Lincoln, *The Birds of Alaska*, 1959

ACROSS THE LAKE, a wolf howls. It is not so much a howl as a wail, a long lament, not languorous but full-toned and intense. The wolf has a tenor voice. It carries operatically across the lake, dies away, echoes back upon itself.

OooooooooooooooooooooooOOOOooo.

You do not stir, but your skin tingles. Some wild part of you desires to rise up and give answer. But from far away comes a better reply, three high trumpet-like notes on an ascending scale.

Ah! Ah! Ah!

On lakes near and far, the loons, hearing the primordial cry, voice their own response, a tumultuous laughter, ecstatic, echoing across all the hard surfaces of this land of rock and water.

—Paul Gruchow, *Travels in Canoe Country*, 1992

THAT NIGHT IT was still, and in the moonlight the loons began as I had heard them before, first the wild, excited calling of a group of birds dashing across the water, then answers from other groups until the entire expanse of the lake was full of their music. We sat around until long after dark and listened, but instead of becoming quiet as the moon went high, the calling increased and there again was the wild harmony, the music that comes only once a year, when it is spring on Lac la Croix.

—Sigurd F. Olson. *The Singing Wilderness*, 1956

The Embodiment of Loneliness
Alone in the far reaches of the Arctic, a yellow-billed loon unleashes its cry, a call that embodies the solitariness of the bird. (Photo © Tom Walker)

The Common Loon

The common loon is far from a common bird. It was christened with its plain-sounding name due to its wide-ranging migration routes, though the red-throated loon is actually more widespread. However, in Great Britain the common loon is known as the great northern diver or great northern loon, certainly more evocative names that are better suited to this spectacular bird of the northland.

When most North Americans think of loons, it is an image of the common loon that comes first to mind. Flying overhead with its distinctive body shape, riding low in the water, or calling its wild cry, the common loon ranges throughout much of the continent, as well as in northern Europe. It is the common loon that has made its way into our popular culture as a symbol of the wilderness.

In the fall the loon came, as usual, to molt and bathe in the pond, making the woods ring with his wild laughter before I had risen.
—Henry David Thoreau, *Walden*

Rising From the Waves
Up from the waves, a common loon spreads its great wings. The Anishinabeg called the loon mahng *and believed it to be brave of heart. American poet Henry Wadsworth Longfellow likened Hiawatha to a loon in his epic poem* Song of Hiawatha, *calling the hero "Loon Heart."* (Photo © Gary L. Lackie)

"A Great Battleship of a Bird"

*T*he British nature photographer G. K. Yeates marveled over the considerable size of the common loon, calling it "a great battleship of a bird" in his birding travelogue about Iceland, *The Land of the Loon*. He went on to further describe the *himbrimi*, the Icelandic name for the loon:

FROM EVERY ANGLE it is a most inspiring bird—great of size, beautiful of plumage and with a remarkable repertoire of calls which seem exactly to fit both the bird which utters them and the wild country it frequents. They are the sounds which have endeared the loon to the Canadian backwoodsman and the *himbrimi* to the Icelandic farmer—a satanic yelling, which sounds like a chorus of all the devils in hell and defies description.

Paragon of Beauty

*O*rnithologist W. L. Dawson poetically depicts the loon and its grace in the water in *The Birds of California* from 1923:

THE LOON IS a paragon of beauty. Alert, supple, vigorous, one knows himself to be in the presence of the master wild thing, when he comes upon a loon on guard in his native element. The bird seems to move without effort, a single backward kick of one of those immense paddles serving to send it forward at any desired speed, while the head is turned inquiringly from side to side as if to take your measure. A short, false, motion, the flash of a gun, and the wild thing has vanished, leaving scarcely a ripple to mark its recent resting place. It reappears, if at all, at surprisingly great distance, and if really alarmed only the head is thrust out of water to take breath, get bearings, and disappear again.

"Proof of their Aversion to Society"

*E*xplorer Samuel Hearne described "Northern Divers" in his bestiary cataloging the wildlife he sighted during his remarkable journeys across Canada. Sent by the Hudson's Bay Company in 1769 in search of a saltwater channel to the west and a fabled copper mine, he chronicled his three-year adventure in *A Journey from Prince of Wales Fort in Hudson Bay to The Northern Ocean*, published in London in 1795:

THESE BIRDS, THOUGH common in Hudson's Bay, are by no means plentiful; they are seldom found near the sea coast, but more frequently in fresh water lakes, and usually in pairs. They build their nests at the edge of small islands, or the margins of lakes or ponds; they lay only two eggs, and it is very common to find only one pair and their young in one sheet of water; a great proof of their aversion to society. They are known in Hudson's Bay by the name of Loons. They differ in species from the Black and Red throated Divers, having a large black bill near four inches long; plumage on the back of a glossy black, elegantly barred with white; the belly of silver white; and they are so large as at times to weight fifteen or sixteen pounds. Their flesh is always black, hard, and fishy, yet it is generally eaten by the Indians.

The Noble "Diver"

*I*celand has been called the Land of the Loon for the many loons that haunt its coast. In an account of travels around Iceland in 1863, English author Sabine Baring-Gould described the northern country's namesake bird:

THE DIVER IS a noble bird; its dark plumage has a metallic lustre; the head and neck are black or green, according to the light in which they are seen; one broad white collar surrounds the neck, beneath the chin is a thread of white like the commencement of a second collar; the black of the body is flecked with white, as though the bird were dressed in magnificent black lace over white. The eye is of a blood-red colour. The bird swims with great celerity, and it is hopeless attempting to come up with it in a boat; it rarely lands, as its short legs thrown beyond the point of equilibrium in the body almost preclude its walking, yet are calculated to give great propelling force in the water. It can remain below the surface for a considerable time, and when it rises, if alarmed, it will keep its body submerged, the dark head alone showing. As one comes suddenly on the diver in a lone tarn [lake], its harsh

Mating For Life
A pair of common loons swim through the reflections of a birch forest. Loons are believed to be one of the few bird species that typically remain with one partner throughout their lifespan, although some new research has found incidences of "infidelity." Males often arrive on summer breeding lakes before the females.
(Photo © Gregory M. Nelson)

loud cry, like the howl of a wolf mixed with jeering bursts of laughter, or the screams of a man in distress, is sufficiently startling.

CHICKS BORN FROM BENEATH THE WING

*A*dult loons are often seen carrying their chicks on their backs or under their wings as they swim. This behavior has given rise to odd beliefs and legends concerning the loon's anatomy and how the female gives birth. In some regions of the world, people believed that loons hatch chicks from a hole under their wings and carry the young hidden beneath their wings until they are old enough to venture forth.

One naturalist writer, the Rev. Lucas J. Debes, recorded such a belief held in the Faeroe Islands in his book *Description of Foeroe, Englished by John Storpen, 1674*: "In Faroe Isles, people believe it hatches its young from a hole formed by nature under its wing. The bird has two holes, one under each of its wings, capable to hold an egg, wherein they (the natives), suppose it hatcheth its eggs, till the young ones come out, neither is it ever seen with more or less than two young ones, which conceit seems not unreasonable."

More than two centuries later, American naturalist John Burroughs scoffed at such beliefs, reporting that "Scotch fishermen will tell you that the loon carries its egg under its wing till it hatches. One would say they are in a position to know; their occupations bring them often into the haunts of the loon; yet the notion is entirely erroneous."

Perhaps one of the oddest and indeed most evocative and terrifying legends that builds on the widespread belief that loons hatch their young from under their wings is this story from the Seneca tribe of western New York state, collected by ethnologists Jeremiah Curtain and J. N. B. Hewitt for the Smithsonian Institution, and published as *Seneca Fiction, Legends and Myths* in 1910–1911. It tells of an evil cannibal spirit known as Deadoeñdjadases. This evil spirit protects his own heart by keeping it hidden beneath the wing of a loon. This story also reflects the awe-inspired mystery many people harbored toward the loon:

Common Loon Nest
A common loon nest resting above the waterline and holding the typical clutch of two eggs. Although it is rare for both parents to leave a nest, at times they do both go off in search of food. Loons may also abandon a nest—and their eggs—if disturbed by humans or natural conditions. (Photo © Gregory M. Nelson)

In his travels he met a mole, and he asked to borrow the mole's skin. He shrank himself in size to fit into the fur, and then continued on.

Further along the journey, he met a sentinel who told him where to go and how to destroy the cannibal. The sentinel said: "The man who dwells in that long lodge is called Deadoeñdjadases. He goes around the world every day, seizing and killing people, whose bodies he brings home to eat. Living in the lodge with him are three sisters, who are all great witches. Every day they are engaged in preparing human flesh and pounded green corn, for their ferocious brother will eat nothing else. Neither Deadoeñdjadases (nor his sisters, for that matter) has a heart in his body; and no one can kill them by beating or cutting them up, for their lives are in another place. In the corner of the lodge is a bed; under this bed is a lake; in this lake a loon swims about; and under the right wing of this loon are the four hearts (the lives) of Deadoeñdjadases and his sisters. The largest heart is his own, the next in size is that of his eldest sister, and the smallest is that of his youngest sister. If you squeeze these hearts their owners will faint away; but if you crush them they will die."

With this sage advice, the Seneca boy dressed as a mole tunneled into the lodge and under the bed. He then changed himself back into a boy and captured the loon, taking the four hearts of the evil cannibal spirits and crushing them. His people were free.

AN EVIL CANNIBAL was terrorizing the Seneca people, carrying them off and devouring them. A Seneca boy had lost several of his friends and relations to the cannibal, and he vowed to put an end to the spirit. He asked his grandmother to make him four pairs of moccasins for the long journey to the abode of the cannibal far away in the east.

1

Audubon Print of Common Loons
Above: *Artist John James Audubon illustrated the common loon in winter (swimming, at left) and summer plumage in his magnificent collection,* The Birds of America.

Winter Plumage
Left: *As with Arctic, Pacific, and yellow-billed loons, common loons molt their flight feathers only once a year, which differs from the red-throated loon, which undergoes the typical avian biannual molting. This common loon wears its winter plumage, a plain-looking variation on the loon's dramatic black-and-white summer plumage.* (Photo © Rob Simpson)

Hiding Posture on Nest

As a stray, unknown loon flies overhead, a nesting common loon lowers itself to hide. This posture also allows the loon to slip quickly from the nest into the water. (Photo © Gregory M. Nelson)

THE LOON COMES TO WALDEN POND

The doyen of American naturalists, Henry David Thoreau, reveled in the call of the loon, just as he reveled in all of nature. Writing in his *Journal*, he recounts his joy at the loon's seasonal return to Walden Pond:

1845–1847: THE LOON comes in the fall to sail and bathe in the pond, making the woods ring with its wild laughter in the early morning, at rumor of whose arrival all Concord sportsmen are on the alert, in gigs, on foot, two by two, three by three, with patent rifles, patches, conical balls, spy-glass or open hole over the barrel. They seem already to hear the loon laugh; come rustling through the woods like October leaves, these on this side, those on that, for the poor loon cannot be omnipresent; if he dive here, must come up somewhere. The October wind rises, rustling the leaves, ruffling the pond water, so that no loon can be seen rippling the surface. Our sportsmen scour, sweep the pond with spy-glass in vain, making the woods ring with rude charges of powder, for the loon went off in that morning rain with one loud, long, hearty laugh, and our sportsmen must beat a retreat to town and stable and daily routine, shop work, unfinished

70

jobs again.

Or in the gray dawn the sleeper hears the long ducking gun explode over toward Goose Pond, and, hastening to the door, sees the remnant of a flock, black duck or teal, go whistling by with outstretched neck, with broken ranks, but in ranger order. And the silent hunter emerges into the carriage road with ruffled feathers at his belt, from the dark pond-side where he has lain in his bower since the stars went out.

And for a week you hear the circling clamor, clangor, of some solitary goose through the fog, seeking its mate, peopling the woods with a larger life than they can hold.

For hours in fall days you shall watch the ducks cunningly tack and veer and hold the middle of the pond, far from the sportsmen on the shore,—tricks they have learned and practiced in far Canada lakes or in Louisiana bayous.

The waves rise and dash, taking sides with all waterfowl.

Oct. 8, 1852. P.M.—Walden. As I was paddling along the north shore, after having looked in vain over the pond for a loon, suddenly a loon, sailing toward the middle, a few rods in front, set up his wild laugh, and betrayed himself. I pursued with a paddle and he dived, but when he came up I was nearer than before. He dived again, but I miscalculated the direction he would take, and we were fifty rods apart when he came up, and again he laughed long and loud. He managed very cunningly, and I could not get within half a dozen rods of him. Sometimes he would come up unexpectedly on the opposite side of me, as if he had passed directly under the boat. So long-winded was he, so unweariable, that he would immediately plunge again, and then no wit could divine where in the deep pond, beneath the smooth surface, he might be speeding his way like a fish. He had time and ability to visit the bottom of the pond in its deepest part. It was as well for me to rest on my oars and await his reappearing as to endeavor to calculate where he would come up. When I was straining my eyes over the surface, I would suddenly be startled by his unearthly laugh behind me. It was commonly a demoniac laughter, yet somewhat like a water-bird, but occasionally, when he had balked me most successfully and come up a long way off, he uttered a long-drawn unearthly howl, probably more like a wolf than any other bird. This was his looning. As when a beast puts his muzzle to the

ground and deliberately howls; perhaps the wildest sound I ever heard, making the woods ring; and I concluded that he laughed in derision of my efforts, confident of his own resources. Though the sky was overcast, the pond was so smooth that I could see where he broke the surface if I did not hear him. His white breast, the stillness of the air, the smoothness of the water, were all against him. At length, having come up fifty rods off, he uttered one of those prolonged unearthly howls, as if calling on the god of loons to aid him, and immediately there came a wind from the east and rippled the surface, and filled the whole air with misty rain. I was impressed as if it were the prayer of the loon and his god was angry with me. How surprised must be the fishes to see this ungainly visitant from another sphere speeding his way amid their schools!

THE LOON TOTEM

The Anishinabeg tribe is composed of some twenty families, also called clans or totems. Named for mammals, fish, and birds, the clans are said to bear the traits of the animals for which they are named. The five principal clans are those of the Crane, Catfish, Bear, Marten, and Loon.

The people of the Loon totem claim to be the chief or royal family, according to William W. Warren's 1885 *History of the Ojibways, Based Upon Traditions and Oral Statements*: "One of their arguments to prove this position is that nature has placed a color around the neck of the loon, which resembles the royal megis, or wampum, about the neck of a chief, which forms the badge of his honor." The following story, told by Tug-waug-aun-ay, the leader of the Crane family, disputes this:

THE GREAT SPIRIT once made a bird, and he sent it from the skies to make its abode on earth. The bird came, and when it reached half way down, among the clouds, it sent forth a loud and far sounding cry, which was heard by all who resided on the earth, and even by the spirits who make their abode within its bosom. When the bird reached within sight of the earth, it circled slowly above the Great Fresh Water Lakes, and again it uttered its echoing cry. Nearer and nearer it circled, looking for a resting place, till it lit on a hill overlooking Boweting

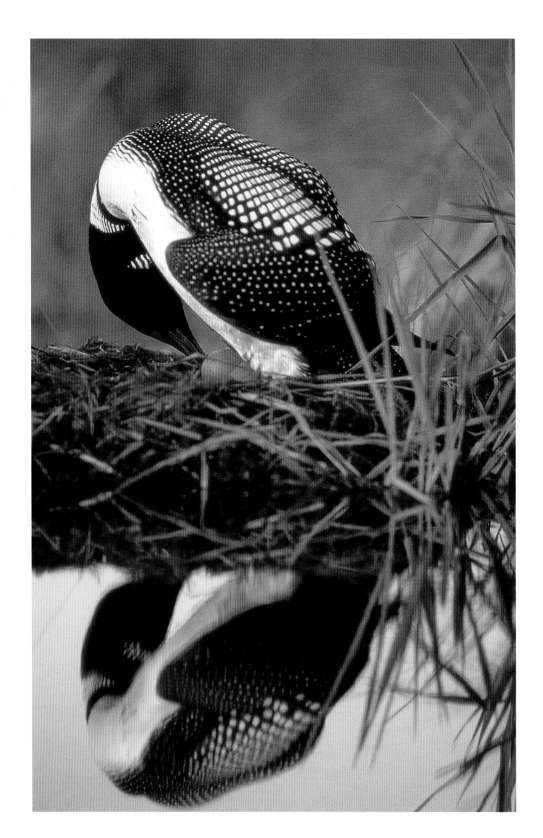

Loon Turning Eggs

Using its beak, a common loon rotates its two eggs on the nest to aid incubation. The normal clutch contains two eggs, and they are typically laid in late spring, often two days apart. The eggs are large and a glossy olive brown in color with dark brown spots. (Photo © Gregory M. Nelson)

Hatching Chick

A common loon chick hatches from its egg after approximately four weeks of incubation. This chick emerged in June in a nest along the shore of Ten Mile Lake in Minnesota. (Photo © Denver A. Bryan)

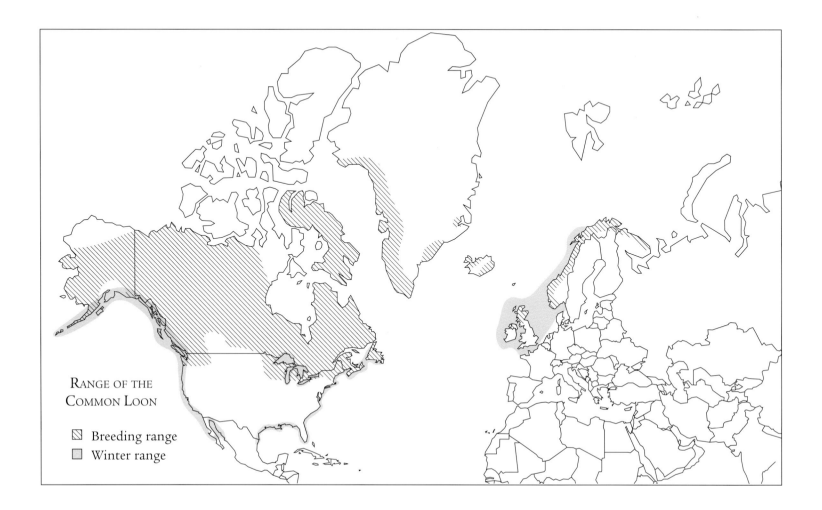

RANGE OF THE
COMMON LOON

☒ Breeding range
☐ Winter range

(Sault Ste. Marie); here it chose its first resting place, pleased with the numerous white fish that glanced and swam in the clear waters and sparkling foam of the rapids. Satisfied with its chosen seat, again the bird sent forth its loud but solitary cry; and the No-kaig (Bear clan), A-waus-e-wug (Catfish), Ah-auh-wauh-ug (Loon), and Mous-o-neeg (Moose and Marten clan), gathered at his call. A large town was soon congregated, and the bird whom the Great Spirit sent presided over all.

Once again it took its flight, and the bird flew slowly over the waters of Lake Superior. Pleased with the sand point of Shaug-ah-waum-ik-ong, it circled over it, and viewed the numerous fish as they swam about in the clear depths of the Great Lake. It lit on Shaug-ah-waum-ik-ong, and from thence again it uttered its solitary cry. A voice came from the calm bosom of the lake, in answer; the bird pleased with the musical sound of the voice, again sent forth its cry, and the answering bird made its appearance in the wampun-breasted Ah-auh-wauh (Loon). The bird spoke to it in a gentle tone, "Is it thou that gives answer to my cry?" The Loon answered, "It is I." The bird then said to him, "Thy voice is music—it is melody—it sounds sweet in my ear, from henceforth I appoint thee to answer my voice in Council."

Thus, the Loon became the first in council, but he who made him chief was the Bus-in-aus-e (Echo Maker), or Crane. These are the words of my ancestors, who, from generation to generation, have repeated them into the ears of their children.

Feeding Time

An adult common loon feeds a minnow to its five-day-old chick. The young loon still wears its soft down. (Photo © Bill Kinney)

The Red-Throated Loon

*T*he red-throated loon differs dramatically from the other four species of loons. From its distinctive and radiant coloration to its diminutive size and unique behavior, it is the nonconformist among the loons.

In addition, the red-throated loon is the farthest ranging, with habitat throughout the northern hemisphere. It winters as far south as the Mediterranean Sea, the coasts of Baja California and Florida, and southern China. If it was not for its trademark red throat, it may well have been better termed the "common" loon.

A loon in a wash
Is as good as a shilling in a
poor man's purse.
—Saying along the coasts of
Norfolk and Suffolk in the
British Isles where the
red-throated loon is believed
to lead the way to the best
fishing spots

Mirror of Water
An adult red-throated loon swims across a mirror of water. In portions of the red-throated loon's range from Norway to the United Kingdom, some people believe that the bird will lead the way to the best fishing sites. (Photo © Tom Walker)

Early Observations on the Red-Throated Loon

Samuel Hearne, during his eighteenth-century journeys in Canada, described the "Red-Throated Divers" he saw along the way from Hudson Bay to the Arctic Ocean:

THIS SPECIES ARE also called Loons in Hudson's Bay; but they are so far inferior to the two former [common and Pacific loons], that they seldom weigh more than three or four pounds. They, like the other species of Loon, are excellent divers; they always feed off fish, and when in pursuit of their prey, are frequently entangled in fishing-nets, set at the mouths of creeks and small rivers. They are more numerous than either of the former, as they frequently fly in flocks; but like them make their nests at the edge of the water, and only lay two eggs, which, though very rank and fishy, are always eaten by Indians and English. The legs of those three species of Loon are placed so near the rump as to be of no service to them on the land, as they are perfectly incapable of walking; and when found in that situation (which is seldom) they are easily taken, though they make a strong resistance with their bill, which is very hard and sharp.

"Like the Plaintive Crying of a Child in Distress"

The red-throated loon ranges around the world, lending its call to the sounds of the northern expanses of several nations. In the vast emptiness of Greenland, the loon's cry can be especially bone chilling, as described by ornithologists Finn Salomonsen and Gitz-Johansen in their guide *The Birds of Greenland*:

OUTSIDE THE BREEDING season the Red-throated Diver is usually silent, but in the summer it has many notes. The ordinary call-note, usually heard in flight, is a resounding, guttural cackling, as *kruck-e-rarrh, kruck-e-rarrh* as a rule rhythmically repeated several times. A variant of this, a short *kruck* or *ock*, is uttered while flying over the breeding-place, when the young are in danger. During courtship display, nest-relief and greeting ceremonies a peculiar note is uttered a long-drawn wail, mournful and eery, which can be rendered as *ooh-eeh*, often uttered in chorus by two or more birds. The Greenlanders usually compare it with the plaintive crying of a child in distress. On a quiet night in the desolate and deserted interior it appears indeed to be the expression of something weird and horrible and may have a blood-curdling effect.

The Ugly Loon Chick

Whereas the adult red-throated loon is a bedazzling beauty of a bird, English ornithologist Kenneth Williamson remarked on the frightful looks of its young. He wrote of the red-throated chick's homeliness in his book, *The Atlantic Islands*, about his bird studies on the Faeroe Islands in the Norwegian Sea:

MOST YOUNG BIRDS, if they are not actually beautiful, at least have some saving grace from ugliness—but not so the young red-throated diver, who is one of the most ungainly creatures I have seen. He was more like some nightmare trick of heraldry than a natural fact, with a brown box of a body, a straight, thick neck and a whitish spectacle-mark which lent a curious reptilian appearance to his head. It was hard to believe that this unlovely creature, by some Cinderella-magic of the wild, would one day achieve the stately beauty of its parents, and slide across the water with the sun fondling its patterned wings and pearl, black-pencilled neck, and shining on the bright red oval of its throat.

Red-Throated Divers by J. G. Keulemann
Left: *The red-throated loon is known in the
United Kingdom as the red-throated diver.
Nature artist J. G. Keulemann illustrated an
adult bird in winter (background, left) and
summer plumage for Henry E. Dresser's* A
History of the Birds of Europe, *published in
1871–1881. (Courtesy of the Minneapolis
Athenaeum at the Minneapolis Public
Library)*

Winter Plumage
The intense red eyes of a red-throated loon appear to shine even brighter against the light grays and whites of the bird's winter plumage. (Photo © Rob Simpson)

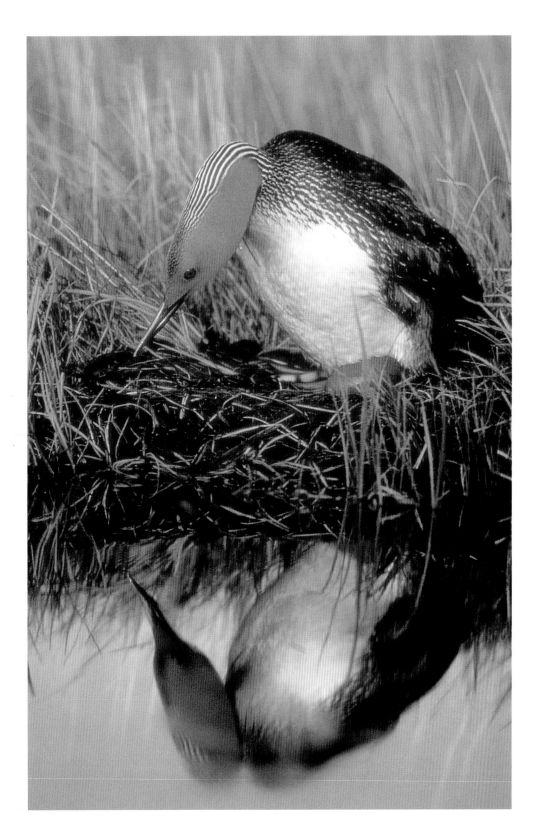

Turning its Egg

Using its beak, a red-throated loon turns its clutch of a single egg to aid incubation. While they are by no means adept on land, red-throated loons have an easier time walking than the other four species of loons, due to anatomical differences. (Photo © Tom Walker)

The Arctic and Pacific Loons

*T*he cry of the Arctic and Pacific loons are perhaps the loneliest loon calls. This is due in part, no doubt, to their habitat—the far northern forests and tundra of North America, Europe, and Asia—which evoke a strong feeling of wildness and solitariness on their own.

The Arctic loon species originally included the Pacific loon, but the two were eventually recognized as separate and distinct species, first by Soviet ornithologists, and in 1985 by the American Ornithologists Union. Today, the Pacific loon lives in North American waters and in parts of the Russian Far East, whereas the Arctic loon ranges across northern Asia and Europe.

Differences between the two species are difficult to discern. Beyond slight variations in size and coloration, most observers comment on the different timbre in the voice of the two species. Whereas the Arctic loon may sound lonely and lost, some believe the Pacific loon sounds as though it is dying or singing its swan song, as it were.

Graceful Head of the Pacific Loon
An adult Pacific loon swims across Alaskan waters. The Pacific loon's plumage is similar to the Arctic loon's, but in summer the Pacific loon's black throat has a purple gloss, whereas the Arctic loon's throat has green highlights. (Photo © Gary L. Lackie)

In addition, unlike the other four species of loons, the Arctic loon species does include one subspecies. The east Siberian Arctic loon (*Gavia arctica viridigularis*) inhabits eastern Russia, from Lake Baikal to the Pacific coast.

"THE MELANCHOLY WHISTLE"

Maud D. Haviland was struck by the call of the Arctic loon, referred to in this excerpt by the British term black-throated diver, while traveling on Siberia's Yenesei River in 1914. She recorded her experiences in *A Summer on the Yenesei*, writing that "their melancholy cries seemed quite in keeping with the loneliness of the place":

I HAD MET with the black-throated diver in Scotland, but there I never heard more of its language than an uncouth shriek. But, on the Yenesei, I constantly heard a beautiful modulated whistle, two or three times repeated, as wild and as far reaching as the call of some wading bird. In fact it seemed such an incongruous sound to proceed from the "ga-garra's" grotesque body that, although I frequently suspected the blackthroat, I never really solved the mystery of its authorship until one day when lying watching duck beside a lake in the tundra, a pair of divers flew towards me, unsuspecting, and pitched in the water about two hundred yards away. They began to play about the tarn, chasing each other, diving beneath the surface, and swimming side by side along the shore. Frequently, with rigid necks and tilted bills, they uttered this weird, melancholy whistle, which was audible for a mile or more. I think it must be the love-song of their kind.

Black-Throated Diver by J. G. Keulemann
Called the Arctic loon in North America, the bird is known as as the black-throated diver in the United Kingdom. Nature artist J. G. Keulemann illustrated an adult "diver" in summer plumage for Henry E. Dresser's A History of the Birds of Europe, *published in 1871–1881. (Courtesy of the Minneapolis Athenaeum at the Minneapolis Public Library)*

THE LOON WITH A BELLY-ACHE

In the 1920s, ornithologist Alfred Marshall Bailey traveled with the Inuit by kayak and dogsled through much of Arctic Alaska in search of loons. He wrote of his exploits at Wainwright Inlet on the far northern coast of Alaska, where he found Pacific loons:

THE CHARACTERISTIC NOTES of the loons sounded clear and resonant, somewhat like a 'Klaxon horn' muffled by distance. The wailing 'oh-o-o-oh' of the Pacific Loon could occasionally be heard, the mournful sound evidently recalling to our Eskimo a case of poisoning in the village a few nights previous, for he stirred in his sleeping bag and muttered, 'Um, him got belly-ache.'

THE MAJORITY OF [bird] collectors in the north have been impressed with the heart-breaking wailing of the Pacific loon. If ever a species enjoyed spreading sorrow through the bird world, it is this loon; Throughout the day The crying may be heard, and when a bird is startled, it lets out a piercing shriek as it dives from view. [One explorer] relates that his cook heard a Pacific Loon calling and rushed back to camp with the report that he had heard the groaning of a dying man, far back on the tundra.

THE HAUNTING VOICE

Naturalist writer Theodora Stanwell-Fletcher wrote of her encounters with Pacific loons during her travels in British Columbia in the 1940s, recounted in *Driftwood Valley*:

Arctic Loon Taking Flight
Beating its wings to gain lift, an adult Arctic loon runs across the water off the Isle of Foula in the Shetlands. Once in the air, loons are graceful, powerful fliers, capable of traveling long distances. But takeoff is another matter, requiring a long stretch of water and much frenzied effort before a loon can become airborne.
(Photo © Gunter Ziesler [Bruce Coleman Ltd.])

Audubon Print of Pacific Loons
Artist John James Audubon illustrated the Pacific loon in winter (swimming, at center) and summer plumage in his book, The Birds of America. *Some historians believe he may have modeled his illustration on European birds, which would be classified today as Arctic loons, but at the time the two species were viewed as one.*

EVERY DAY NOW across the still green waters . . . we hear the voice of the Pacific loon—that ghostly, haunting, wailing "oh-h-h, oh-h-h-h, ooh-ooh." Like a woman crying hopelessly, endlessly. Like a baby bear who has lost its mother. Like the faint far-off foghorn of a ship at sea. Like the mournful sigh of wind in a pine tree. We have a pair staying with us for a time. . . . When they're separated they begin calling and answering in those voices which haunt one day and night, and of which, one can never hear enough.

EARLY OBSERVATIONS OF THE PACIFIC LOON

Samuel Hearne, the sixteenth-century explorer in the service of the Hudson's Bay Company, described the Pacific loons he saw along the way from Canada's Hudson Bay to the Arctic Ocean:

THIS SPECIES IS more beautiful than the [common loon];

HUNTING THE LOON

Hunting loons for food as well as for their skin and feathers to be used for clothing was common among many native cultures. Edward S. Curtis described how the Inuit cooked loons and loon eggs in his mammoth work *The North American Indian*: "The flesh of birds, either fresh or dried, is eaten usually with oil, or perhaps cooked in a dock-leaf soup. Bird-eggs are consumed either in raw or cooked state." Yet the loon proved difficult quarry for even the most skilled native hunter. As they were such a challenge to hunt, many non-native sportsmen later shot loons for fun, including artist John James Audubon. Loons would dive—seemingly at the instant that an arrow or bullet was fired, as described by hunters and explorers:

THE METHOD USUALLY adopted by the Indians to kill [the loon], is by fixing a large bough at the head of the canoe, to conceal themselves till they paddle near the place where they are; when at a convenient distance, they fire, though not always with success. In the Chippeway language it is called a maunk, which agrees with the French word manquer, to fail; it being, from its shyness, very difficult to kill. The skin, which is very tough and thick, is dried and made use of as cases to cover their guns, to prevent the wet from spoiling them.

—J. Long, *Voyages and Travels of an Indian Interpreter and Trader*, 1791

LOONS ARE ABUNDANT in the water and are on the Indians' list of Ducks, therefore good food. They are wonderfully expert at calling them. This morning a couple of Loons appeared flying far to the east. The Indians at once began to mimic their rolling *whoo-ooo-whoo-ooo*; doing it to the life. The Loons began to swing toward us, then to circle, each time nearer. Then all the callers stopped except Clawhammer, the expert; he began to utter a peculiar cat-like wail. The Loons responded and dropped their feet as though to alight. Then at 40 yards the whole crew blazed away with their rifles, doing no damage whatever. The Loons turned away from these unholy callers, and were none the worse, but wiser. This scene was repeated many times during the voyage. When the Loons are on the water the Indians toll them by flashing a tin pan from the bushes behind which the toller hides till the bird is in range. I saw many clever tollings but I did not see a Loon killed.

—Ernest Thompson Seton, *The Arctic Prairies: A Canoe-Journey of 2000 miles in search of the Caribou*, 1911

having a long white bill, plumage on the back and wings black, elegantly tinged with purple and green, and prettily marked with white spots. In size they are equal to the former; but are so watchful as to dive at the flash of a gun, and of course are seldom killed but when on the wing. Their flesh is equally black and fishy with the former, but is always eaten by the Indians.

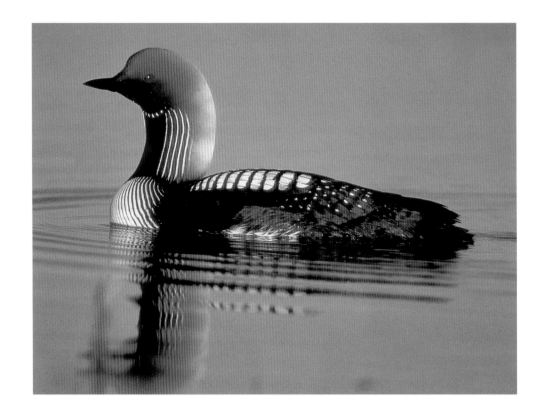

Mirrored by the Water
Swimming above its own reflection on an Alaskan lake, a Pacific Loon basks in the summer sun. (Photo © Tom Walker)

Nesting Arctic Loon
An adult Arctic loon incubates its eggs on a nest in June near Dalarna, Sweden. Nests are built close to the water's edge, usually on islands in lakes. Males do most of the initial nest building, often in the exact position of the previous year's nest site. (Photo © Janos Jurka [Bruce Coleman Ltd.])

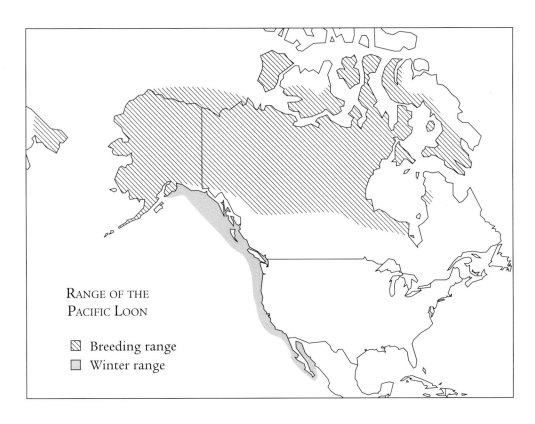

RANGE OF THE
PACIFIC LOON

⬚ Breeding range
⬚ Winter range

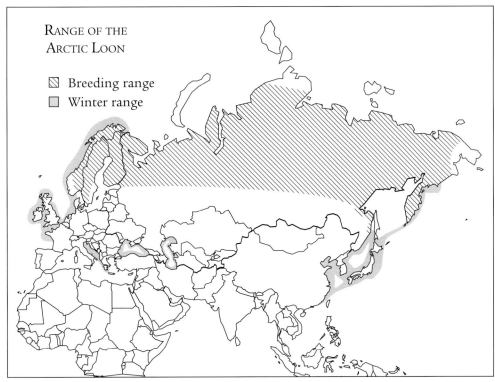

RANGE OF THE
ARCTIC LOON

⬚ Breeding range
⬚ Winter range

The Yellow-Billed Loon

Called him Strong-Heart, Soan-ge-taha!
Called him Loon-Heart, Mahn-go-taysee!
—Henry Wadsworth Longfellow,
"Song of Hiawatha"

At first glance, many mistake the yellow-billed loon for a common loon. The color of the bill is the most distinguishing difference between the two species, but often even the bill color can vary.

Although it is larger than any of the other loons, the yellow-billed loon is also more elusive. This is due in large part to the remoteness of its habitat, stretching along the far northern Arctic coastlines of North America, Europe, and Asia. Thus the yellow-billed loon is perhaps the most mysterious of loons.

Nesting Yellow-Billed Loon
Using its beak, a yellow-billed loon turns its eggs during incubation. In comparison to the common loon, the yellow-billed loon typically has fewer and larger white streaks in its necklace. (Photo © Tom Walker)

First Recorded Sighting of the Yellow-Billed Loon

The yellow-billed loon may have been christened with its scientific name, *Gavia adamsii*, in error. The name was bestowed on the loon in 1859 by British zoologist G. R. Gray in honor of Edward Adams, a British naval surgeon, polar explorer, and collector of natural history specimens. Gray believed Adams "discovered" the species in the mid-1800s during a voyage to the Canadian Arctic, while traveling in the footsteps of one of the several British polar expeditions led by Sir John Franklin in the early 1800s.

Explorer and scientist Dr. John Richardson accompanied Franklin on his original polar journey of 1825–1827 and documented in the group's journals his sighting of the bird that became known as the yellow-billed loon. Thus, Richardson may have been the true "discoverer" of the yellow-billed loon—"discoverer" at least from a European point of view.

Franklin's polar expedition was sponsored by the British admirality to chart the Arctic coast from Alaska's Point Barrow to Canada's Mackenzie River Delta and east to Coronation Gulf. Coming to the end of the journey at the mouth of the Coppermine River, Richardson spotted what he at first believed was a common loon but later realized was a yellow-billed loon:

IN MY WAY I had occasion to wade through a small lake, when two birds, about the size of the *northern diver*, and apparently of that genus, swam, with bold and angry gestures, to within a few yards of me, apparently very impatient of any intruder on their domain. Their necks [beaks] were of a beautiful pale yellow colour, their bodies black with white specks. I consider them to belong to a species not yet described, and regretted that, having left my gun at the tents it was not in my power, to procure one of them for a specimen.

"A Roar of Wings"

Ornithologist Alfred Marshall Bailey was one of the first to research and describe the yellow-billed loon in detail,

Showing its Wings
A large, adult yellow-billed loon spreads out its wings to their full extent, flapping them vigorously to shed excess water from the feathers. (Photo © Gary Schultz)

reporting on the species in the 1920s. He writes here about his observations on the far northern coast of Alaska:

WITH A COUPLE of Eskimos and a skin canoe . . . we lined along the shore of Wainwright Inlet, a dog team furnishing the power. Few [yellow-billed loons] were seen until about eight miles up the inlet, where I secured a fine adult. The inlet here is at least half a mile wide, with several prominent points, and as we progressed a flock of a dozen birds swam from the shadows and, taking wing, soon disappeared toward the distant shore. From then until dusk we had an unusual opportunity to observe these rare birds, for they were continually rising before us and alighting far ahead. To give an accurate estimate of their numbers would be impossible, for we probably saw many individuals again and again, but at one time, when a flock arose with a roar of wings, we counted thirty birds milling over the surface of the inlet. I have never before seen as many loons of any species so congregated.

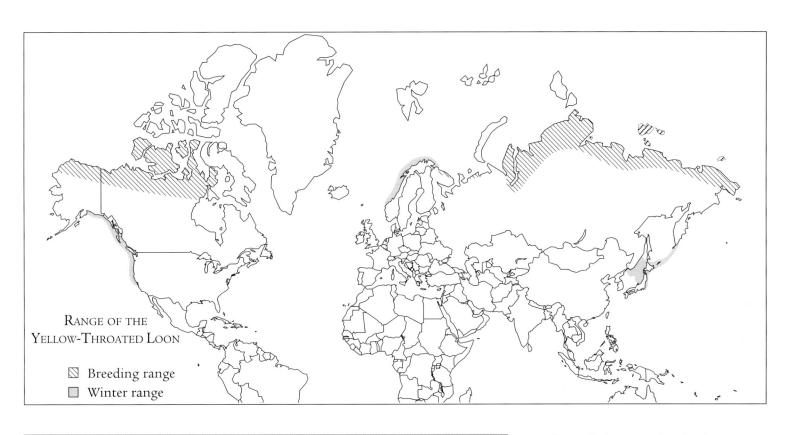

RANGE OF THE
YELLOW-THROATED LOON

⬚ Breeding range
⬚ Winter range

Yellow-Billed Loon and Reflection
The yellow-billed loon is typically the largest of all loons. Its overall average dimensions are nearly the size of a Canada goose. (Photo © Tom Walker)

Loonskin Parkas and Garments

As loons had adapted to the Arctic with their warm, waterproof plumage, native people adapted loons to various uses. The most common human use of loons was as food, but loonskins—with or without feathers—were also used to make clothing and hats. Seventeenth-century explorer Samuel Hearne described the uses of loons in the Canadian Arctic:

The skins of those birds are very thick and strong, and they are frequently dressed with the feathers on, and made into caps for the Indian men. The skins of the Eagles and Raven, with their plumage complete, are also applied to that use, and are far from being an unbecoming head-dress for a savage.

Ornithologists Alexander Wilson and Charles Lucian Bonaparte described in *American Ornithology* a variety of garments made from loonskins throughout the loon's Arctic range:

The Barabinzians, a nation situated between the river Ob and the Irtisch, in the Russian dominions, tan the breasts of this and other water fowl, whose skins they prepare in such a manner as to preserve the down upon them, and, sewing a number of these together, they sell them to make pelisses, caps, &c. Garments made of these are very warm, never imbibing the least moisture, and are more lasting than could be imagined.

The natives of Greenland use the skins for clothing, and the Indian about Hudson's Bay adorn their heads with circlets of their feathers.

The Laplanders cover their heads with a cap made of the skin of a loom, (loon) which word signifies in their language lame, because the bird cannot walk well. They place it on their head in such a manner, that the bird's head falls over their brow, and its wings cover their ears.

The Inuit of Alaska and the Arctic reaches of Canada also employed loonskins to fashion their primary outerwear: parkas. The following excerpts describe the parkas of the Inuit and how they were crafted:

Both sexes wear the parka, a frock-like garment reaching to the knees. The pattern is similar for both men and women, excepting that there is an open seam on each side of the bottom hem of the women's parka. Parkas intended for outdoor wear have an attached hood which is pulled over the head or allowed to remain folded at the back of the neck. Indoor parkas are lighter in weight. Parkas are made of bird-skins (duck, gull, or loon) or of animal-skins (caribou [now reindeer], mink muskrat, or squirrel). The waterproof parka for use in rainy weather, in choppy seas when in kaiaks, or while hunting, is made of seal-intestine.

—Edward S. Curtis, *The North American Indian*, 1930

The garments worn by the men consist of a skin frock, which is put on over the head and has a hood variously bordered by strips of skin. These borders are made usually of an outer strip of wolfskin with the long hairs standing out like a halo, as before described. Just within this is sewed another belt or band of skin from the wolverine so that the long outer hairs lie back against the wolfskin border, producing a pleasing contrast. These halo like borders, when the hood is drawn up, surround the face and give a picturesque appearance to the wearer. The back of the hood is made usually of several pieces sewed in such a way as to take the form of the head. A gore usually extends from the top of the shoulders at the base of the hood down on each side of the chest, and is generally of white-hair skin from the belly of the reindeer. The sleeves and lower border of this garment are fringed with a narrow band of wolf or wolverine skin. These garments may be made of the skins of wild or tame reindeer, Parry's marmot, muskrats, mink, or waterfowl, such as cormorants, auklets, murres, eider ducks, or loons, and in the region southward of the Yukon mouth the skins of emperor and white-front geese are also used for this purpose. One such garment is made from the skins of scaup ducks, with the hood of Parry's marmot skins, and is bordered around the bottom with a narrow fringe of wolfskin. On the lower Yukon very poor people utilize even the skins of salmon for making their frocks.

—Edward William Nelson, *The Eskimo About Bering Strait*, 1896–1897

Inuit Loonskin Parka

A parka crafted of the head and neck sections of yellow-billed loons, believed to be of Inuit manufacture from the early twentieth century. The loonskin was cured to retain the feathers, and while the skin is thin and pliable, offering easy movement, the feathers provide a thick layer of insulation. Early Arctic explorers reported these loonskin parkas to be warm as well as waterproof. This parka was sewn with sinew; the cuffs are edged with caribou fur; and the neck, front opening, and jacket bottom are trimmed with the fur of either a wolf or lynx. (Courtesy of the Ethnology Program, Provincial Museum of Alberta, Edmonton)

The Future of the Loon

The loon's voice, those wild callings.
What is it this creature is trying to tell us?
What is it we so need to hear?
—Literary biologist Jeff Fair

Imagine the wilderness without the loon's song. The northern woods and lakes would suddenly become as silent as the grave.

Yet on many lakes the loon's cry is being overwhelmed by the resounding noise of speedboats, fishing craft, and personal watercraft—the sounds of human beings at play. Our use of lakes for recreation continues to grow at an alarming rate, encroaching on the loon's habitat.

In addition, we adjust water levels on lakes to suit our recreational desires and manufacturing needs. We refashion nature with beaches, terraces, and new tree plantings to match our idea of wilderness. Human beings are condemned to art, and all of this threatens the survival of the loon—no matter how good our intentions and sometimes in ways we do not understand.

The future of the loon is by no means assured. But there is still hope, as literary biologist Jeff Fair outlines below.

Common Loon and Reflection
Mirrored in the water, a common loon swims across a Michigan lake at daybreak. The plight of the loon also reflects the future of the environment and our own survival. Through the centuries, the loon's call was heard as a warning of stormy weather; today, the silencing of that call on many lakes throughout the world is a modern warning call of a new environmental storm. (Photo © Gregory M. Nelson)

Romancing the Loon

*F*or eighteen years, independent biologist and writer Jeff Fair has studied loons under boreal skies from Maine to Alaska for federal agencies, power companies, environmental organizations—and himself.

A SEEMINGLY WELL-BEHAVED loon under close observation can slip below the water's surface in the middle of a large lake on a calm and brilliant day—and never be seen again. This is not unusual, and any loon biologists whose field notes don't from time to time include the word "disappeared" are cheating their science. Most of us learn to tolerate, accept, even celebrate such gavian indiscretions.

Much of our attraction to the loon, after all, derives from its clandestine behaviors. Nothing like a taste of the unknown, the mysterious, to haunt the human mind with intrigue and inspire it toward romance. But there is a dark side to our romance with the loon. Today we suffer a powerful and unrequited longing for this wild spirit on lakes from which it has disappeared completely, driven off by human meddling or poisoned out by toxins we have dealt upon the landscape.

Is it possible that the common loon, this stable creature with a low center of gravity and sixty million years of evolutionary fine-tuning, signature voice and spirit of our northern wilds, symbol of this vast and haunting land which the entire continent once thought was inviolable, is disappearing from its haunts? Quite so.

After thrilling the night for millennia with territorial cries throughout the boreal forest and as far south as Pennsylvania, Illinois, and Iowa, loons had quietly disappeared northward by 1976, to breeding lakes from New Hampshire through northern Wisconsin. This retreat inspired numerous monitoring and restoration efforts—largely powered by volunteers—across the northern states.

By 1981, the southern Ontario region, described in 1817 as "a vast uninhabited solitude" by naturalist Charles Fathergill, had suffered enough human habits and habitation to turn away its native loon population. This prompted the Long Point Bird Observatory in Port Rowan to form the Ontario Lakes Loon Survey, a network of volunteers later to become the nationwide Canadian Lakes Loon Survey. I asked the present director of the survey, biologist Harry Vogel, about the status of the loon in Ontario. The southern edge of their breeding range is still creeping northward here too, he told me. Why? Well, he said, human behavior.

The behavior of our modern monoculture—the incredible *busyness* we inflict upon our waters—is more significant than habitat loss to shoreline development. Our disturbance of nesting sites by berrypickers, picnickers, part-time naturalists, canoeists and rowboaters, clandestine lovers, anglers, and campers is frequently enough to frighten the loons off of their eggs and dissuade them from returning. Similar human blunders separate adult loons from their chicks, leaving the little ones susceptible to predation or eventual starvation.

Dieter Schoenefeld is a charter member of the Loon Survey, who with his wife Marlies monitors loon populations and reproduction on ten lakes in southern Ontario, including McFarlane Lake on which they live. I inquired about this year's loon tally. "Very disappointing," he said. Fewer than the usual number of chicks. Why? Jet Skis, powerboats, lack of enforcement, campers on the nesting islands, gulls taking the eggs. (Gulls are massing inland to live and breed on freshwater lakes in recent decades, lured there by available food in the form of human garbage.) And what does he see as the future of the loon in southern Ontario? "We are replacing their habitat with ours," he said. "My honest feeling is that there are too many of us."

Exacerbating these injuries, government agencies rush headlong to answer a perceived "need" for developed recreational opportunities—with too little concern for the local wildlife. In Maine, for example, the Federal Energy Regulatory Commission, which requires hydroelectric dam operators to monitor and mitigate their impacts on common loons nesting on the larger reservoirs, also bids the same companies to pave more boat ramps and establish more shoreline campsites. Canadians suffer the same irony. In the fall of 1993, the Ontario Ministry of Natural Resources erected six tent platforms, a picnic table, and an outhouse adjacent to a loon nesting site on Charleston Lake, just across from Jim Willis' island cottage. Willis was incensed. His family had been in the area since 1784. "We have respected these loons for

Nesting Red-Throated Loon
A red-throated loon incubates its eggs on a nest along an Alaskan lake. Shoreline development and fluctuating water levels threaten loon nesting sites in many parts of the bird's range. Human disturbance of nesting sites also frequently frightens loons off their eggs, and some never return. (Photo © Tom Walker)

decades," he explained. He and neighbors wrote letters to the agency regarding its mistake. They maintained pressure. In the spring of 1994, ministry workers dismantled the entire campsite.

"The love of this lake and the responsibilities that go with it have been handed down in my family from generation to generation," Willis told me. "Now it is time to pass it along to my son, Damian." I asked Damian, age sixteen, why he too had recently joined the Loon Survey. "The loons are beautiful animals," he said. "I didn't want to see them leave."

Even our last frontier has not escaped the onslaught. Nancy Tankersley, a wildlife biologist with the Alaska Department of Fish and Game, has documented the steady disappearance of loons from lakes in Anchorage and the Matanuska–Susitna Valley north of town. I asked her how this was possible.

"Same as everywhere else," she said. "Loss of nest sites to lakeside development—and human disturbance. Two hundred and fifty thousand people play here. We have firecrackers, free-running dogs, fishing, swimming, boating." I asked her if the Jet Ski had reached Alaska. She rolled her eyes. "In droves," she said. "They could be the death knell for these loons." Alaskans are, in organizational membership at least, a very environmental crowd. They take great pride in their landscape and wildlife. But as Tankersley points out, it only takes a few transgressors. "And they play pretty hard up here."

Nor is human disturbance of the loons confined to the more heavily developed areas of our north country. "The myth that Canadians love to perpetuate is one of a great big vast country with its population snuggled up on the southern border, and the rest of it just this pristine wild country," Kevin McNamee, Acting Executive Director of the Canadian Nature Federation, told me. "In reality, there's a fairly strong amount of development in the hinterlands." Logging and mining development entail road building; roads mean access; access facilitates recreation. Etc.

Some of the biggest changes he sees have occurred in that middle ground of cottage country, where small cottages now give way to permanent homes with their ancillary equipment tied up at large floating docks: the inboard power boat, the Jet Ski. "The machinery that people use for recreation has become bigger, faster, and noisier," McNamee said. "And ev-

ery once in a while you see a loon floating around in that pool of technology."

But cottage country has a conscience too. Dick Weber, for example, a "summer Canadian" from Washington state keeps a cottage on Thirty-one Mile Lake in Quebec, due west of Algonquin Provincial Park. Through his interest in the loon's call he became a member of the Loon Survey, organized his neighbors, and eventually assumed the chair of the North American Loon Fund. The Fund is a continent-wide organization dedicated to the conservation of loons, which also coordinates the efforts of affiliates such as the Survey. "We not only monitor loon numbers here," Weber told me, "we monitor our behavior, too."

Then there are the poisons. Acid-killed lakes support no loons. Partially acidified lakes support loons, but these birds seem to produce fewer fledglings. The pattern appears simple: Acidic waters contain fewer fish, therefore less loon food, leading to a more critical competition between young siblings. The weaker chick misses food, weakens, and eventually lags behind to starve. Over half of North America's loons breed on lakes susceptible to acid damage—primarily on the Canadian Shield.

Heavy metals, mercury and lead in particular, poison loons via the nervous system, incapacitating the victim by reducing vision and coordination, causing it to weaken from starvation until, unable to hold its head above water, it drowns. Mercury is associated with acidification, leaching from the earth into lakes where it accumulates in the upper level of the food web—the fish eaters (eagles, loons, humans). Mercury may also invoke an "estrogenic" effect in which less than fatal concentrations fiddle with gender and sexuality in embryonic males, producing adults lacking the proper hardware or desire to carry out reproductive functions. Biologists estimate that twenty-nine thousand loon pairs are at risk in Ontario alone. One-sixth of the loons sampled recently around northern New England and the Great Lakes carried levels of mercury known to reduce reproductive success in other waterfowl. Yes, but does it affect loons in this way? We don't know for sure, but there are indications. On a sample of lakes monitored for over a decade by Wisconsin Loon Watch volunteers, the number of loon pairs has increased over the past seven years, but fewer chicks have hatched.

Lead arrives primarily in the form of fishing sinkers, picked up by a loon along with the gravel used to grind up fish in the foregut. How common can this be? In a recent New England study 52 percent of autopsied loons had died from lead poisoning. Eight of thirty-six loon carcasses found on heavily used recreation lakes in Canada in 1994 carried the lead sinkers that had poisoned them to death.

The U.S. Environmental Protection Agency and the Canadian Wildlife Service have taken stands against the manufacture and sale of smaller lead sinkers, but related legislation has gone nowhere in either the U.S. Congress or the Canadian Parliament. Great Britain banned lead sinkers years ago to protect their swans, but American legislatures bear on with their common inertia, ignoring the plight.

Lead can also arrive from a point source, namely the barrel of a .30-30, as I was reminded a few years ago by a semiretired, semisodden fishing guide in the backwoods of Labrador. "Best way to teach a loon to stay off my trout," he explained. No use arguing. I left his name with an interested Mounty at the railhead. Loons are protected by Canada's Migratory Birds convention, the U.S. Migratory Bird Treaty Act, and state and provincial wildlife laws, and though a few disgruntled fishermen still shoot at them, most outdoors folk today enjoy the loons and their music as part of the ambience. Many realize that loons have fed themselves on excellent fishing lakes for thousands of years without harming the fishery.

Monofilament fishing line left in the water ensnares loons, crippling wings and twisting shut bills, leading to slow starvation. Fishline entanglement is the second leading cause of adult loon mortality in New Hampshire. This summer in Alaska, three of the twenty-nine loons captured for color banding wore the scars of monofilament restraint. These were the survivors.

Loons winter on coastal waters south to Mexico, and oil spills, commercial fishing nets, and who knows what other toxins threaten them. Uncertainty abounds; too little is known for the good of loons. In a recently published, two-decade-long study, the U.S. Fish and Wildlife Service reports that half the red-throated loons in Alaska have disappeared. No one can say why.

Still there is hope. Vigilante networks across the conti-

nent monitor and foster the loons' survival. Under the ministrations of New Hampshire's Loon Preservation Committee, the leader and elder of this clan, a threatened population of common loons has doubled in size. But numbers alone do not secure the future. I asked Committee chairman Jordan Prouty for his outlook. He did not appear very smug.

"We've beaten human disturbance, raccoons, and gulls," he said, "and now we have mercury to worry about. And public access. Where does it end?"

Well sir, it doesn't. Even the water itself, when regulated behind a dam, can wreak havoc at the loon's nest. A six-inch increase in water level during the twenty-eight-day incubation period can flood the nest; a twelve-inch drop can strand the nest too far inland. Such fluctuations are particularly common on hydroelectric projects. A number of hydro reservoirs across the U.S. have instituted new water-level management schemes and other programs to lessen these effects. I wondered about Canada. I phoned Ontario Hydro headquarters and asked if anyone is looking into the effects of their water management on loons. "If we aren't, we should be," one biologist said, and promised to call me back if they were. No one called. Then I thought of the granddaddy of all hydros, the proposed Great Whale complex, growing like cancer up there on the cheek of James Bay on the southern edge of Hudson Bay.

I decided to call on an expert on the region—Margaret Cromarty, a full-blooded Cree who lives at Chisasibi on the eastern shore of James Bay, at the bottom end of the La Grande hydro complex. I inquired about her credentials. "Raised in the bush and still live in the bush," she said. I asked her about loons.

"They used to be a delicacy for us, but we don't eat them much anymore."

"Why not?"

"We were told they have mercury, like the fish," she said. "And there's not so many now." She remembers seeing huge flocks on the water a generation ago. But not anymore.

I asked about the meaning of the loon in her culture. "The Crees hold it in high regard," she said. I pressed her further, hoping to hear some old legend, some lost and lovely story, but she offered none. Instead, like Jim Willis, she thought of her children.

"They don't know what a loon is," she said. "They hardly hear it anymore. They only know the dollar coin. They need to know the loon's spirit."

"And what is the loon's spirit?" I asked.

She was silent for a moment. Then she said, "You can hear it in its voice."

The loon's voice, those wild callings. What is it this creature is trying to tell us? What is it we so need to hear?

I am sitting on the doorsill of a little outpost cabin among the low and pointy timber of this distant, dismal, beautiful, brooding north country. A boreal lake, purple in the twilight, lies before me. The cool air off the water carries a brew of essences: black spruce and sphagnum, water and earth. Above a lush and ringing silence, the loons' voices echo. Maddened cries from hell? I think not. Arpeggios of loneliness? Not that either. I listen. And I do not feel alone.

An other-worldly sound? Hardly. It feels quite fitting and essential to this one, in the judgment at least of one tired but contented biologist crouching at his threshold with a tin cup of warm whisky in his paw.

What are they saying out there? A difficult and personal question, but I'll answer it. Through our science—our modern mythology—we are remaking the ancient loon legends. Once again the loon is forecasting a storm, this time an environmental storm, portended by the poisons in its tissues and that regretful hush over our soured lakes. Once again the loon offers us vision, this time of ourselves, our actions, our own future. What I hear are gentle warnings. Reminders. Perhaps enough of us will listen. Perhaps we will heed these storm-calls, maintain the wild character of our north country, and avoid the terrible silence.

Loon With Chick
A common loon chick rides on the back of a parent through a reedy bay. Human disturbance of nests may also separate adult loons from their chicks, leaving the little ones susceptible to predation or eventual starvation, endangering future gavian generations. (Photo © Gregory M. Nelson)

Sources and Suggested Readings

Audubon, John J. *Ornithological Biography.* 5 vols. Edinburgh: A. Black, 1831–1839.

————. *The Birds of America.* New York: Geo. R. Lockwood and Son, 1870.

Audubon, Maria, ed. *Audubon and his Journals.* 2 vols. New York: Dover Publications, 1986. First published by Charles Scribner's Sons, 1897.

Bailey, A. M. "A report on the birds of northwestern Alaska and regions adjacent to Bering Strait." 1926.

Baring-Gould, Sabine. *Iceland: Its Scenes and Sagas.* London: Smith, Elder and Co., 1863.

Bent, Arthur Cleveland. *Life Histories of North American Diving Birds.* Washington, DC: U.S. National Museum Bulletin 107, 1919.

Bly, Robert. "The Loon's Cry." *Selected Poems.* New York: Harper & Row, 1986.

Brinton, Daniel G. *Myths of the New World.* New York: Leypoldt and Holt, 1868.

Burton, Robert. *Bird Behavior.* New York: Alfred A. Knopf, Inc., 1985.

Crowley, Kate, and Mike Link. *Love of Loons.* Stillwater, Minn.: Voyageur Press, 1987.

Curtin, Jeremiah, and J.N.B. Hewitt. *Seneca Fiction, Legends, and Myths: Part 1*, vol. 32. Washington, DC: Smithsonian Institution Bureau of American Ethnology, United States Government Printing Office, 1910–1911.

Curtis, Edward S. *The North American Indian*, vol. 20. New York: Johnson Reprint Corporation, 1930.

Dawson, W. L. *The Birds of California.* San Diego: South Moulton Company, 1923.

Debes, Rev. Lucas J. *Description of Foeroe, Englished by John Storpen, 1674.*

Dement'ev, G. P., and N. A. Gladkov, editors. *Birds of the Soviet Union*, vol. 2. Jerusalem: Israel Program for Scientific Translations, 1968.

Dennis, Roy. *Loons.* Stillwater, Minn.: Voyageur Press, 1993.

Densmore, Frances. *Chippewa Customs*, bulletin 86. Washington, DC: Smithsonian Institution Bureau of American Ethnology, United States Government Printing Office, 1929.

Dresser, Henry E. *A History of the Birds of Europe,* vol. 8. London: Henry E. Dresser, 1871–1881.

Dwyer, Corinne A. *Loon Legends.* St. Cloud, Minn.: North Star Press, 1988.

Erdoes, Richard, and Alfonso Ortiz, eds. *American Indian Myths and Legends.* New York: Pantheon, 1984.

Fair, Jeff. "Last Call?" *Equinox.* Sept./Oct. 1994.

Farnham, Thomas J. *Travels in the Great Western Prairies.* London: Richard Bentley, 1843.

Forbush, Edward Howe. *Birds of Massachusetts and Other New England States. Part I: Water Birds, Marsh Birds and Shore Birds.* N.p.: Massachusetts Department of Agriculture, 1929.

————. *The Natural History of the Birds of Eastern and Central North America.* Boston: Houghton Mifflin Company, 1939.

Franklin, J. *Narrative of a Second Expedition to the Shores of the Polar Sea in the Years 1825, 1826, and 1827 Including an Account of the Progress of a Detachment to the Eastward by John Richardson.* London: John Murray, 1828.

Gabrielson, Ira N., and Frederick C. Lincoln. *The Birds of Alaska.* Harrisburg, PA: The Stackpole Company; Washington, DC: Wildlife Management Institute, 1959.

Garber, Clark M. *Stories and Legends of the Bering Strait Eskimos.* Boston: The Christopher Publishing House, 1940.

Greij, Eldon. "Taking a Dive." *Birder's World*, June 1995.

Gruchow, Paul. *Travels in Canoe Country.* Boston: Bulfinch Press, 1992.

Hale, H. "Huron Folklore." *Journal of American Folk Lore*, vol. 1. New York: G.E. Stewart & Co., 1888.

Haviland, Maud D. *A Summer on the Yenesei.* London: Edward Arnold, 1915.

Hearne, Samuel. *A Journey from Prince of Wales Fort in Hudson Bay to the Northern Ocean.* London, 1795.

Huxley, J. S. "Courtship Activities of the Red-throated Diver." *Journal of the Linnaean Society of London* 35 (1923).

Klein, Tom. *Loon Magic.* Ashland, Wisc.: Paper Birch Press, Inc., 1985.

Kohl, Johann Georg. *Kitchi-Gami: Life Among the Lake Superior Ojibway.* London: Chapman and Hall, 1860. Reprinted by the Minnesota Historical Society Press, 1985.

Leeming, David Adams, and Margaret Adams Leeming. *Encyclopedia of Creation Myths.* Santa Barbara, Calif.: ABC–CLIO, Inc., 1994.

Lewis, Meriwether. *History of the Expedition of Captains Lewis and Clark 1804-5-6*, vol. 2. Chicago: A.C. McClurg & Co., 1905.

Long, Charles H. *Alpha: The Myths of Creation.* New York: George Braziller, 1963.

Long, J. *Voyages and Travels of an Indian Interpreter and Trader Describing the Manners and Customs of the North American Indians with an Account of the Posts Situated on the River Saint Laurence, Lake Ontario, &c.* London: privately printed for the author, 1791.

Maher, Ramona. *The Blind Boy and the Loon and Other Eskimo Myths.* New York: The John Day Company, 1969.

Mason, Michael H. *The Arctic Forests.* London: Hodder and Stoughton, Ltd., 1924.

McIntyre, Judith W. *The Common Loon: Spirit of Northern Lakes.* Minneapolis: University of Minnesota Press, 1988.

Nelson, Edward William. *The Eskimo About Bering Strait.* Washington, DC: Smithsonian Institution Bureau of American Ethnology Volume 18, United States Government Printing Office, 1896–1897.

Norman, Howard. *Northern Tales: Traditional Stories of Eskimo and Indian People.* New York: Pantheon Books, 1990.

Ogburn, Charlton. *The Adventure of Birds.* New York: William Morrow, 1975.

Olson, Sigurd F. *Listening Point.* New York: Alfred A. Knopf, Inc., 1958.

_____. *The Singing Wilderness.* New York: Alfred A. Knopf, 1956.

Rasmussen, Knud. *The People of the Polar North.* 1908.

Roberts, Thomas S. *The Birds of Minnesota*, 2nd ed., vol. 1. Minneapolis: University of Minnesota Press, 1936.

Salomonsen, Finn, and Gitz-Johansen. *The Birds of Greenland.* Copenhagen: Ejnar Munksgaard, 1950.

Saunders, Howard. *Manual of British Birds.* London: Gurney and Jackson, 1927.

Savage, Candace. *Wings of the North: A Gallery of Favorite Birds.* Minneapolis: University of Minnesota Press, 1985.

Seton, Ernest Thompson. *The Arctic Prairies: A Canoe-Journey of 2000 miles in Search of the Caribou. Being the Account of a Voyage to the Region North of Aylmer Lake.* New York: The Scribner Press, 1911.

Slater, Henry H. *Manual of the Birds of Iceland.* Edinburgh: David Douglas, 1901.

Stanwell-Fletcher, Theodora. *Driftwood Valley.* Boston: Little, Brown and Company, 1946.

Swainson, Rev. Charles. *The Folk Lore and Provincial Names of British Birds.* London: Elliot Stock, 1886.

Turner, Lucien M. *The Hudson Bay Eskimo: Ethnology of the Ungava District, Hudson Bay Territory*, vol. 11. Washington, DC: Smithsonian Institution Bureau of American Ethnology, United States Government Printing Office, 1889–1890.

Warren, William W. *History of the Ojibways, Based Upon Traditions and Oral Statements*, vol. 5 of the Collections of the Minnesota Historical Society. Saint Paul: Minnesota Historical Society Press, 1885. Reprinted by the Minnesota Historical Society Press in 1984.

Williamson, Kenneth. *The Atlantic Islands.* London: Routledge & Kegan Paul, 1948.

Wilson, Alexander, and Charles Lucian Bonaparte. *American Ornithology; or the Natural History of the Birds of the United States*, vol. 4. Edinburgh: Constable and Co., 1831.

Wood, W. *New England Prospectus.* 1634.

Yeates, G. K. *The Land of the Loon: Being the Experiences of a Bird-Photographer on Two Visits to Iceland in Search of the Great Northern Diver.* London: Country Life Limited, 1951.

Acknowledgments

Thanks are due to the following people who helped in the preparation of this book, listed here in alphabetical order: Roy Dennis; Jeff Fair; Michael Greaves of Alfred A. Knopf; Eldon Greij, publisher and editor of *Birder's World* magazine; Eric Hanson; Edward R. Kukla of the Minneapolis Public Library Special Collections Department; Judith W. McIntyre; Robert Mosimann of the University of Minnesota Press; Anna Pappalardo of the University of British Columbia Museum of Anthropology; Tim Ready of the Science Museum of Minnesota; and Mike Rensner of Colin Baxter Photography Ltd.

Index

Organizations Working for Loons

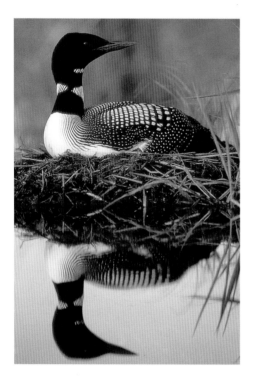

Nesting Loon
A common loon rests on its nest during the four weeks of incubation. Both males and females share nest-building duties, as well as incubating eggs and finding food. (Photo © Gregory M. Nelson)

Defenders of Wildlife
1244 Nineteenth Street NW
Washington, DC 20036 USA

North American Loon Fund
6 Lily Pond Road
Gilford, NH 03246 USA

Ontario Lakes Loon Survey
Long Point Bird Observatory
P.O. Box 160
Port Rowan, Ontario
Canada N0E 1M0

Common Loon Protection Project
Maine Audubon Society
Route 1, Box 118
Falmouth, ME 04105 USA

Minnesota Loon Preservation Project
506 Torrey Building
314 Superior Street
Duluth, MN 55802 USA